OSPREY AIRCRAFT OF THE ACES • 25

Messerschmitt Bf 110 *Zerstörer* Aces of World War 2

SERIES EDITOR: TONY HOLMES

OSPREY AIRCRAFT OF THE ACES · 25

Messerschmitt Bf 110 *Zerstörer* Aces of World War 2

John Weal

First published in Great Britain in 1999 by Osprey Publishing
Elms Court, Chapel Way, Botley, Oxford, OX2 9LP

ISBN 1 85532 753 8

Edited by Tony Holmes
Page design by TT Designs, T & B Truscott
Cover Artwork by Iain Wyllie
Aircraft Profiles by John Weal
Figure Artwork by Mike Chappell
Scale Drawings by Mark Styling

Origination by Valhaven Ltd, Isleworth, UK
Printed through Bookbuilders, Hong Kong

99 00 01 02 03   10 9 8 7 6 5 4 3 2 1

EDITOR'S NOTE
To make this best-selling series as authoritative as possible, the editor would be extremely interested in hearing from any individual who may have relevant photographs, documentation or first-hand experiences relating to the elite pilots, and their aircraft, of the various theatres of war. Any material used will be fully credited to its original source. Please write to Tony Holmes at 10 Prospect Road, Sevenoaks, Kent, TN13 3UA, Great Britain.

ACKNOWLEDGEMENTS
The author wishes to acknowledge the provision of photographs from Dr Alfred Price and Aerospace Publishing for use in this volume.

BIBLIOGRAPHY
ADLER, MAJOR H., *Wir greifen England an!* Wilhelm-Limpert Verlag, Berlin, 1940
ANTTONEN, OSSI and VALTONEN, HANNU, *Luftwaffe Suomessa – in Finland 1941-44 Vol 1*. Helsinki, 1976
BINGHAM, VICTOR, *Blitzed!, The Battle of France, May-June 1940*. Air Research Publications, New Malden, 1990
BONGARTZ, HEINZ, *Luftkrieg im Westen*. Wilhelm Köhler Verlag, Minden, 1940
COLLIER, RICHARD, *Eagle Day*. Hodder and Stoughton, London, 1966
CULL, BRIAN, et al, *Twelve Days in May*. Grub Street, London, 1995
DETTMANN, FRITZ, *40.000 Kilometer Feindflug*. Im Deutschen Verlag, Berlin 1940

(*bibliography continued on page 103*)

CONTENTS

THE EARLY SUCCESSES

For the third time in less than ten minutes a British heavy bomber filled his sights. Carefully, at little more than wave-top height, the young leutnant eased his twin-engined Bf 110 up into position directly astern of the labouring Wellington. There was no sign of life from the rear turret. He moved in even closer, before opening fire. Flames erupted from both wings of the stricken bomber as the punctured tanks spewed fuel. With an almost imperceptible dip of its nose, the Wellington wallowed into the sea and, to use the leutnant's own words in later describing the action, 'immediately sank like a stone'.

He circled the oil slick that marked the bomber's last resting place on the sea bed some 25 km off Borkum, westernmost of the German East Frisian Islands, in a vain search for survivors. A light sea-mist was already beginning to gather as the dark-green Bf 110 set course for the mainland. Within 15 minutes the fighter was roaring in low over the hangars of Jever airfield, its wings rocking to indicate an unprecedented success – three RAF bombers downed in a single sortie – to the cheering crowds below.

The date was 18 December 1939, and Luftwaffe fighters had just inflicted a major defeat upon the enemy. In a series of short, sharp clashes spread over 30 minutes across some 150 km of the North Sea (since dubbed the 'Battle of the German Bight'), the defenders claimed the destruction of no fewer than 38 of the attacking bombers. Although actual RAF losses were to prove far fewer, they were nonetheless severe enough to finally convince Bomber Command of the folly of unescorted daylight attacks on German targets.

The true significance of the 18 December 'Battle' has since come to be measured not in the number of immediate RAF casualties, but in the fundamental effect it had on British bombing policy. Henceforth, with but a few, well-publicised, exceptions, Bomber Command's offensive against Germany would be carried out only under the cover of darkness.

Although the defending Luftwaffe fighters had been a mixed force of Bf 109s and Bf 110s, the latter had played a prominent, if not dominant part. Thus, the machine which was arguably the most successful fighting aircraft to emerge from the recent campaign against Poland (and the one which had certainly been the most respected by its Polish counterparts), had now – in an entirely new role in defence of the Reich – been instrumental in delivering a swingeing, strategic defeat on the RAF. The original, somewhat contentious, concept which had given rise to the *Zerstörer* appeared fully vindicated. And the Bf 110's continued success now seemed assured . . .

Although the Luftwaffe had first differentiated between *'leichte' Jagdgruppen* and *'schwere' Jagdgruppen* (i.e. 'light' fighter wings and 'heavy' fighter wings) as early as 1937, such a distinction initially had little meaning. Both types of unit flew the same aircraft and performed virtually the same duties. It was not until 1 November 1938 – a scant ten months before the outbreak of World War 2 – that redesignation of the 'heavy' *Gruppen* heralded a final parting of the ways between the two.

At that time all Luftwaffe unit designations consisted of three digits, the first indicating the seniority of the unit, the second its function and the third the command to which it was subordinated. Thus, for example, JG 132 identified itself as being the first (1) fighter formation (3) within LwGrKdo 2 (2). Now, however, the middle digit '3' would refer specifically to 'light' fighter units, the 'heavies' being allocated the number '4' as their new middle digit designator.

Exactly a third of the new fighter force was affected by these changes, the seven 'new' *schwere Jagdgruppen* thus created being;

LwGrKdo 1:

I.(s)/JG 141	(ex-II./132)	Jüterbog-Damm
II.(s)/JG 141	(ex-III./132)	Fürstenwalde

LwGrKdo 2:

I.(s)/JG 142	(ex-I./134)	Dortmund
II.(s)/JG 142	(ex-II./134)	Werl
III.(s)/JG 142	(ex-IV./134)	Lippstadt

LwGrKdo 3:

I.(s)/JG 143	(ex-II./234)	Illesheim

LwGrKdo 4:

I.(s)/JG 144	(ex-III./334)	Gablingen

There was also an eighth *schwere Jagdgruppe*, this having been activated as such on 1 September 1937 as part of the Luftwaffe's *Lehrgeschwader* (tactical evaluation group). Designated I.(s.J)/LG 1, this unit was tasked with testing the heavy fighter prototypes produced in response to the specifications issued by the RLM, and evaluating their operational potential.

The original intention had been for 'light' fighters to be controlled by regional *Luftgauen* (air districts) for homeland defence duties, while the *schwere Jagdgruppen* would be placed under operational commands to carry out a variety of strategic and offensive roles such as long-range fighter suppression, bomber escort, strike and ground attack.

On 1 May 1939 the introduction of a new and simplified system of unit designation throughout much of the Luftwaffe finally did away with the clumsy 'light' and 'heavy' fighter nomenclature. As of that date the latter became *Zerstörer* (literally 'destroyers', which was a term borrowed from the navy). At the same time, two further *Zerstörergruppen* were activated from hitherto *leichte Jagdgruppen*. This was to be just the beginning of a major expansion programme which, by the spring of 1942, foresaw a *Zerstörer* arm consisting of 16 complete *Geschwader* – some 3000 machines in all!

However, the outbreak of hostilities four months later brought an abrupt halt to this ambitious scheme. At the start of World War 2, the

The first *Gruppe* to be equipped with the Bf 110C was I.(Z)/LG 1, the operational trials unit based at Barth on the Baltic coast. As with any new aircraft entering service for the first time, the Bf 110 was beset by a number of small technical problems, as this photograph clearly shows – the cowlings have been removed to allow the groundcrew better access to the troublesome port DB 601 engine of aircraft L1+A12 of 2. *Staffel*

Upon the outbreak of the war two of the three Bf 110-equipped *Zerstörergruppen* still had Jumo-powered B models on strength. Here, *Bertas* of 2./ZG 1 are flying escort for a *Stukagruppe* en route to Warsaw on 8 September 1939

Luftwaffe's *Zerstörer* arm still comprised just the ten *Gruppen* mentioned on the previous page. And of those ten, only three were equipped with their proper aircraft!

The winning design selected to become the Luftwaffe's future heavy fighter, or *Zerstörer*, was Dipl.-Ing. Willi Messerschmitt's Bf 110, the prototype of which had first flown on 12 May 1936. Despite some dissenting voices among the RLM's Technical Department against the feasibility of such a 'maid-of-all-work' machine, the concept of a strategic heavy fighter capable of 'holding its own' deep within enemy airspace captured the imagination of the Luftwaffe's Commander-in-Chief, Generalfeldmarschall Hermann Göring. Under such august patronage development forged ahead, but production was hampered by the lack of a suitable powerplant. The shortcomings of the prototype's Daimler-Benz DB 600 series engine meant that early production models had to be fitted with lower-powered Junkers Jumos, which were not considered adequate for combat use.

It was not until the DB 601

Posing proudly in front of his new Bf 110C, Hauptmann Günther Reinecke, *Gruppenkommandeur* of I./ZG 76, models the lightweight overalls favoured by many early *Zerstörer* crew members. But note, too, the small Bf 110 silhouette on the engine upper cowling (extreme left). Previous published captions of in-flight shots of Bf 110s have often referred to this as the 'shadow of the wingman's aircraft', which is patently not the case. The exact significance of these painted silhouettes (which may also just be made out on L1+A12 above) is, however, not known engine was finally awarded clearance for service use late in 1938 that the *Zerstörer* production programme could properly justify its 'highest priority' rating. In January 1939 the first Bf 110Cs were delivered to I.(Z)/LG 1 at Barth, where they quickly began to supplant the unit's earlier Jumo-powered B-models. In the following spring and early summer, I./ZG 1 and I./ZG 76 likewise started to take delivery of the improved *Cäsar* to replace their own recently-acquired Bf 110Bs. These would be the only three *Zerstörergruppen* flying the Bf 110 upon the outbreak of war in September. Despite the rapidly gathering momentum of Bf 110C production (manufacture was now also being carried out by both Focke-Wulf and Gotha), the remaining seven *Zerstörer* units would all still be equipped with Bf 109s when hostilities commenced.

Unlike the high-profile Bf 109, which had been paraded before the world's press whenever the opportunity arose – and especially during the regular bouts of sabre-rattling which preceded Hitler's every fresh territorial demand – the Bf 110 made very few pre-war public appearances. Indeed, its first, and last, such 'demonstration of force' was the transfer of I.(Z)/LG 1 to Dresden-Klotzsche at the time of the German occupation of Czechoslovakia in March 1939. Three months later the same *Gruppe* participated in a ceremonial fly-past over Berlin.

Towards the end of August 1939 a similar event took I.(Z)/LG 1 to East Prussia to overfly the famous World War 1 memorial at Tannenberg. Ostensibly part of a commemorative celebration, this move was, in reality, a ruse to disguise the *Zerstörers'* transfer to Jesau, in East Prussia, in preparation for the forthcoming attack on Poland.

POLAND

Reportedly upon the direct intervention of Hermann Göring himself, the Luftwaffe threw its entire twin-engined *Zerstörer* strength (all 90 serviceable machines!) into the assault on Poland. The Bf 110s were divided almost equally between the three *Zerstörergruppen* involved. These *Gruppen* were, in turn, deployed at almost equidistant intervals along Germany's common borders with Poland, each being positioned to lend direct support to one of the three main axes of advance.

Bf 110 UNITS IN THE POLISH CAMPAIGN

Luftflottenkommando 1 (North) HQ: Stettin/Pommerania

		Base	Type	Est-Serv
1. Fliegerdivision (Schönfeld/Crössinsee)				
I./ZG 1	Maj Joachim Huth	Mackfitz	Bf 110B/C	34-27
Luftwaffen-Lehrdivision (Jesau/East Prussia)				
I.(Z)/LG 1	Maj Walter Grabmann	Jèsau	Bf 110C	33-32

Luftflottenkommando 4 (South) HQ: Reihenbach/Silesia

		Base	Type	Est-Serv
2. Fliegerdivision (Grottkau)				
I./ZG 76	Hptm Günther Reinecke	Ohlau	Bf 110B/C	35-31
		Total		102-90

This ZG 76 crew, seen scrambling aboard their machine, are also dressed in the summer-pattern overalls. The point of interest illustrated here is the fact that *Zerstörer* pilots wore seat-pack parachutes, while the rear crew member was equipped with a back-pack type

In the south-west, the Silesian-based I./ZG 76 provided the sole fighter escort for *2. Fliegerdivision's* three *Kampfgeschwader* of He 111 and Do 17 bombers, whose twin tasks it would be to clear paths for the ground forces advancing on Cracow as well as north-eastwards to invest the Polish capital, Warsaw, from the south.

In Pommerania, I./ZG 1 would be likewise employed covering *1. Fliegerdivision's* bombers and Stukas as they struck eastwards across the Polish Corridor, before swinging south-east to threaten Warsaw from the north.

On the far side of the Corridor, in the Reich's isolated province of East Prussia, I.(Z)/LG 1 formed the fighter component of the *Luftwaffen-Lehrdivision*, whose four *Kampfgruppen* would spearhead the advance due

Another DB 601 requiring attention. The mechanics of ZG 1 have already rigged up a block and tackle, while two small boys (right foregroupn) have parked their bikes and await further developments with interest. Just visible on this 1. *Staffel* machine are two thin white bands encircling the rear fuselage (below the port rudder). This was a tactical marking worn by both Bf 110s and Bf 109s during the campaign in Poland

south out of encircled East Prussia. Again, the ultimate objective was the enemy's capital.

All three *Zerstörergruppen* had been scheduled to escort their divisional bombers on a series of pre-emptive strikes against Polish Air Force bases and installations during the opening hours of the campaign. However, when 1 September 1939 dawned, a heavy and persistent ground mist was covering much of northern Poland. Only Hauptmann Reinecke's I./ZG 76 down in the south was able to fly their mission as planned . . . or nearly so.

Their orders called for an 0600 take-off to cover the He 111s of I. and III./KG 4 during a raid on the Polish airfield at Cracow. Given the historic nature of the mission – the first of the war for both the *Zerstörer* and the bombers – and the need for the two formations to rendezvous from their separate bases some 120 km apart, precise timing should have been of the utmost importance. Yet if a postwar account of the operation, penned by the then Oberleutnant Wolfgang Falck, *Staffelkapitän* of 2./ZG 76, is to be believed, he and his pilots suddenly decided to steal a march on the other members of the *Gruppe* by taking off an hour early!

If 2./ZG 76 were hoping that this ploy would enable them to claim the first aerial victory of World War 2, they were to be disappointed. This distinction went to a neighbouring dive-bomber unit (see *Osprey Combat Aircraft 1 – Junkers Ju 87 Stukageschwader 1937-41* for details). In fact, Falck's pilots spent a fruitless 60 minutes, not finding their charges until they arrived over the target. Completely unopposed, each *Gruppe* of Heinkels duly unloaded 48 tons of bombs on a deserted Cracow and turned for home – most Polish Air Force units had vacated their peace-time bases and dispersed to prearranged satellite fields in the hours leading up to the invasion (see *Osprey Aircraft of the Aces 21 – Polish Aces of World War 2* for details).

On the return flight Falck's *Staffel* realised they were running low on fuel, which was, perhaps, not to be wondered at under the circumstances. As they neared the German frontier they left the bombers and set a direct course back to Ohlau. It was at this juncture that Falck spotted a lone, high-winged aircraft far below the 4000 m altitude at which the Heinkel formation had been flying.

Diving to investigate, he was rewarded with a warning burst of fire from the vigilant rear-gunner of a Heinkel He 46 army reconnaissance machine. A few minutes later Falck chanced upon another singleton, this time a low-winged monoplane with a large, spatted, fixed undercarriage. As he moved in closer the machine banked away and he caught a momentary glimpse of red near its wingtip.

Prior to the outbreak of hostilities, Luftwaffe aircrew had been briefed that the Poles were toning down the distinctive red and white checker-board national insignia on some of their aircraft. They were overpainting the high-visibility white areas to leave just the skeletal red sections showing. Convinced that the machine twisting and turning in front of him was a Polish PZL P.23 Karas light bomber, Falck let fly. Fortunately for his intended victim, Falck's aim was poor. From close range he recognised the unmistakable bent-wing shape of a Ju 87 Stuka. The angular marking on its wingtip was the aircraft's individual identity letter – a red 'E'.

Falck's later reporting of this incident led to such markings being over-painted in black – later still, in the campaign against Russia, many Luftwaffe units eschewed red *Staffel* markings altogether to avoid confusion with the Soviet star. Although he had seen the red letter on the upper surface of the Stuka's wing, Falck's apparent failure to notice the black *Balkenkreuz*, thinly edged in white, alongside it was proof of the inadequacy of the Luftwaffe's own national insignia when seen in plan view.

Many other pilots made the same mistake in these first days, and before long oversized crosses – often of full-chord width – began to adorn the wings of Luftwaffe machines engaged in the air war over Poland. Nor was Falck's confusing the Ju 87 for an enemy PZL P.23 an isolated incident. The basic similarity in layout of these two aircraft when observed from certain angles produced a rash of other such cases of misidentification.

Although the crews of I./ZG 76 had completed their first full day of operations without gaining a single kill, their luck was to change 24 hours later. The total lack of aerial opposition on 1 September prompted Generalmajor Bruno Loerzer, AOC *2. Fliegerdivision*, to assign just one of Hauptmann Reinecke's *Staffeln* to escort the full might of KG 4 on a raid against Deblin the following morning. Situated 90 km south of Warsaw, Deblin was a major communications centre ringed by three airfields.

Although they encountered heavy flak over the target area, the 88 He 111s reported no sign of enemy air activity. Released from their close escort duties, one *Schwarm* (section of four aircraft) of Bf 110s winged over into a steep dive. They had spotted a number of Polish machines dispersed on one of the fields which had escaped damage from the bombing. Despite the intense light flak, each Bf 110 made several strafing runs, cannon and machine guns blazing. It was all over in a matter of minutes. When the four *Zerstörer* climbed back up to rejoin the retreating bombers, they left behind eleven burning wrecks to mark their passing.

That same afternoon 1. and 2./ZG 76 were ordered to fly a *freie Jagd* (literally a 'free hunt', or fighter sweep) over the Lodz region. Here they encountered the Polish Air Force for the first time when they were attacked head-on by half-a-dozen PZL P.11c fighters. A fierce dogfight ensued, and although Oberleutnant Nagel and Leutnant Lent each claimed the destruction of one of the gull-winged Polish machines, I./ZG 76 were to lose three of their own number in this day's fighting.

Helmut Lent, who had participated in the earlier ground-strafing at Deblin, was one of several future aces who scored their first kills with I./ZG 76 in Poland. Another was the highly-decorated, but relatively little-known, Austrian Gordon Mc Gollob – the 'Mc' in Mc Gollob was not part of a Caledonian family name, but a highly unusual Christian name bestowed upon the young Gollob by his parents. They were both Austrian artists who named their son after an American friend, Gordon Mallet Mc Couch, no doubt to the latter's delight – but to the utter mystification of the Viennese registrar of births, to whom the child's forenames had to be spelled out letter by letter!

Gollob would be the first Luftwaffe fighter pilot to achieve 150 victories, and he was later appointed by Reichsmarschall Hermann Göring to replace the 'disgraced' Adolf Galland as his *General der Jagdflieger* in January 1945. Helmut Woltersdorf, who, like Lent, would go on to find greater fame as a nightfighter *Experte*, also opened his scoreboard with I./ZG 76, claiming two of his eight day victories against the Polish Air Force.

But the *Gruppe*'s highest scorer, with three confirmed kills over Poland, was Wolfgang Falck. His first, on 5 September, was another of the seemingly ubiquitous PZL P.23s, which he despatched near Lodz – the scene of I./ZG 76's first clash with Polish fighters three days earlier. And this time he made quite sure of his opponent's identity before opening fire;

'We were on a *freie Jagd* deep in enemy territory when I caught sight of an aircraft similar to a Ju 87 flying towards us. As it got closer I could see it was a PZL P.23. It passed below us. Slamming the throttles shut, I heaved my machine into a tight turn and dived onto its tail. I could make out the red and white checkerboards on its wings and tail quite clearly. The Polish gunner began firing at me, but his shots went wide; the tracers flashing past my cockpit. I got him in my sights, made a small correction, and pressed the button. My guns hammered. A small jet of flame appeared. As I pulled up over him he suddenly exploded in a ball of fire.'

On 10 September Falck was summoned to Breslau by Hermann Göring and informed that his *Staffel* had been chosen to provide the escort for the Generalfeldmarschall's Ju 52 during his forthcoming tour of frontline bases. After being briefed on the itinerary, Falck was invited to take coffee with Göring in the latter's personal compartment aboard the luxurious train which served as his travelling HQ. The C-in-C was eager to hear a first-hand report on his *Zerstörers'* baptism of fire over Poland. Falck recounted his experiences to date, which obviously found favour (his unofficially taking off an hour ahead of schedule on the opening day must have been either glossed over or conveniently forgotten). As the *Staffelkapitän* prepared to leave, Göring signalled to an aide. Falck was surprised to be handed a paper bag. In it was an Iron Cross!

Although the Polish campaign still had more than a week to run, enemy opposition in the air was by this time virtually nil. Most Bf 110 crews found themselves flying ground-support missions during the closing stages – a task not always to their liking. I./ZG 76 had claimed 31 enemy aircraft destroyed in combat, 19 of which were subsequently confirmed.

While Major Reinecke's *Gruppe* had been engaged over southern Poland, what of the *Zerstörergruppen* in the north? Of the two, little is known of I./ZG 1's activities other than the fact that they were the least successful of all, and probably suffered the heaviest casualties.

Major Huth's I./ZG 1 was one of the oldest flying units in the Luftwaffe. Its lineage dated back to its original activation as the *'Fliegergruppe Damm'* on 1 April 1935. Since that time it had undergone several changes of designation. As II./JG 132 'Richthofen', it was the first *Gruppe* to be equipped with the Bf 109 fighter. It had then been numbered among the seven *Jagdgruppen* selected to become a 'heavy fighter' and, ultimately, *Zerstörer* unit. When it received its first Bf 110s in the spring of 1939, the event was celebrated in traditional JG 132 manner by the consumption of 110 bottles of *Export-Bier* – just one bottle more than had been quaffed to mark the earlier transition from Ar 68 to Bf 109!

In the last week of August 1939 I./ZG 1, comprising two *Staffeln* of Bf 110Cs and one of Bf 110Bs, departed Damm for Mackfitz, an airfield near Regenwalde, in Pommerania. Here, a few days were lazily spent swimming and playing volley ball before a final briefing on 31 August.

Despite the poor visibility which hampered the first day's operations in the north, I./ZG 1 managed to fly some 35 sorties without incident on 1 September. But 24 hours later Hauptmann *Freiherr von* Müllenheim, *Staffelkapitän* of 3./ZG 1, was killed in action against PZL P.11 fighters – the 'Gods of War' were kinder to *Frhr. von* Müllenheim's naval officer brother, who was destined to be the highest-ranker to survive the sinking of the battleship *Bismarck* on 27 May 1941.

Command of 3. *Staffel* was immediately assumed by Oberleutnant Walter Ehle, who would be credited with two of the six confirmed kills gained by I./ZG 1 over Poland. He, too, would later make his mark in the nightfighter arm. After the seizure of the Polish Corridor, the *Gruppe* transferred to East Prussia. Here, they used the small strip at Mühlen as a

'Well done, that airman, have an Iron Cross!' **The Generalfeld-marschall hands out one of his 'little paper bags' during a tour of front-line units**

By the beginning of hostilities I.(Z)/LG 1's codes were of the standard four-digit type. Wearing just such codes is 'L1+ZB', which was the third of the *Gruppe*'s trio of *Stabskette* machines. This aircraft was normally flown by the Technical Officer, with 'XB' allocated to the *Gruppenkommandeur* and 'YB' to the Adjutant. Note here, too, the *Gruppe*'s 'Wolf's head' badge and the Bf 110 silhouette on the cowling

forward landing ground for subsequent operations, which consisted primarily of escorting Stukas raiding Warsaw. During one such mission, on 6 September, they lost a second *Staffelkapitän* when 1./ZG 1's Major Hammes also fell victim to a PZL P.11 fighter. His replacement was Oberleutnant Martin Lutz, an ex-*Condor Legion* pilot who had already been shot down once in Spain and had lived to tell the tale. He would not be so fortunate a year hence when, as *Kommandeur* of *Erprobungsgruppe* 210 – a specialised fighter-bomber unit – his Bf 110 was brought down by RAF fighters over Dorset.

Despite I./ZG 1's relatively poor showing, their forward base was one of those included in Göring's tour of Luftwaffe units towards the close of the campaign in Poland. During his visit the Generalfeldmarschall praised the *Gruppe*'s efforts and 'doled out Iron Crosses, Second Class, to nearly every member of aircrew'.

As the early aerial clashes over Poland had shown, longevity of service had not guaranteed I./ZG 1 success in the field. More valuable, perhaps, would have been a sounder grasp of the Bf 110, and its operational capabilities. And the unit with such knowledge was I.(Z)/LG 1, the trials evaluation wing which, for the past eight months, had been committed to formulating the proper tactical deployment of the Luftwaffe's new twin-engined *Zerstörer*. Commanded by Major Walter Grabmann (another recent participant in the Spanish Civil War, where he had served as *Kommandeur* of the *Condor Legion*'s *Jagdgruppe*, scoring seven victories in the process), I.(Z)/LG 1 would emerge as by far the most successful of the three *Zerstörergruppen* engaged over Poland.

Things did not get off to a very good start, however. Again bedevilled by the all-pervading fog, the He 111 bombers of II.(K)/LG 1 nevertheless managed to take off from their East Prussian base late on the morning of 1 September. Their objective was Warsaw-Okecie airfield. Such a raid into the enemy's heartland was expected to provoke stiff opposition, and I.(Z)/LG 1 was up in force to provide protection for the Heinkels. Sure enough, several squadrons of the Polish Pursuit Brigade intercepted the

Luftwaffe formation, and despite the Bf 110s' best efforts, six bombers were lost in the running fight which ensued. Grabmann's pilots were able to claim only two elderly PZL P.7s, and the *Kommandeur* himself was wounded in the encounter.

That afternoon the bombers and *Zerstörer* of LG 1 returned to Warsaw. During Major Grabmann's temporary incapacity, I.(Z)/LG 1 was being led by his senior *Staffelkapitän*, Hauptmann Schleif. Some 30+ PZL fighters had been scrambled at the raiders' approach, and as they clawed for altitude, they were spotted by Schleif high above. The heavy Bf 110s winged over into a screaming dive, but the Poles scattered. In the ensuing melée, one of the Messerschmitts was apparently damaged. As it crabbed away it attracted the attention of a Polish fighter, but the 'lame duck' was a decoy. Intent on lining up his victim, the PZL pilot was unaware that he was himself filling the gunsight of Hauptmann Schleif, who was sitting just 80 metres behind his tail. A

Warsaw-Okiece under attack, as seen from the air . . .

short burst of fire blew the PZL apart, and according to contemporary accounts of the engagement, this carefully rehearsed ruse succeeded not once but five times!

Forty-eight hours later, the Bf 110s of I.(Z)/LG 1 again clashed with

. . . and from the ground, as Polish Bomber Brigade PZL P.37 Los medium bombers go up in flames

15

some 30 of the PZLs defending Warsaw, and again they claimed five of the Polish fighters, this time for the loss of one of their own. By the end of the campaign the *Gruppe*'s score had risen to 30 confirmed kills, and although the air war in Poland did not produce a single *Zerstörer* ace (the sole Luftwaffe ace to emerge from the Polish conflict was, in fact, a member of the *Zerstörer* arm, but his unit was one of those still flying the Bf 109 under a temporary *Jagdgruppe* designation – see *Osprey Aircraft of the Aces 11 - Bf 109D/E Aces 1939-41*), two of I.(Z)/LG 1's pilots came close – Leutnant Methfessel and Feldwebel Warrelmann were credited with four victories against the Polish Air Force, adding more later.

In the following paragraphs, Werner Methfessel describes his first kill – one of the PZLs engaged over the Polish capital on the morning of 3 September;

'The weather had finally cleared up, and at 6000 m east of Warsaw, we found ourselves in brilliant sunshine. The city was spread out below us like a model. You could see the streets and squares, the churches and factories. Okecie airfield was clearly visible too.

'It was from there that we saw a swarm of Polish fighters climbing up to meet us. At first just tiny specks in the vastness of the sky, like specimens under a microscope, but gradually getting larger and swimming into focus as they got closer. I counted about 30 of them. High-winged PZLs, with their cranked wings and short, stumpy fuselages looking more and more like a swarm of bees.

'In the meantime, our *Kampfgruppen* had arrived. Passing far below us in a tight formation as if on peacetime manoeuvres. But the Poles didn't bother with them – they appeared only to have eyes for us.

'"Tune in to Radio Warsaw", I said to my wireless-operator. And the cockpit was immediately filled with the strains of a tango – the same melody to which we had danced at Garmisch when the whole *Staffel* had flown down there to celebrate last New Year's Eve. But the music was suddenly interrupted by a shrill voice, and then silence. Leaning forward, I looked down and saw bombs bursting around the city's transmitter masts.

'By now the Polish fighters were only 600 metres below us. I slipped the safety catches off the guns and kept my eye on the *Staffelkapitän*'s machine as we swung slightly eastwards in order to have the sun at our backs when we dived. The leader's wings rocked. That was the signal. Down we went.

'Almost at the same moment the Poles tipped onto their sides and dived back towards the ground too. Our concerted attack quickly degenerated into a series of individual engagements. It was a fantastic sight. The white skeins of machine-gun fire criss-crossed above the city like a giant spider's web. In amongst them dark shadows flickered, dived and weaved. Lower still, the red pin-point explosions of anti-aircraft fire and smoke rising from the wounded city.

'I tried to pick out a target. It was not easy amid all this confusion. But I finally spotted a Pole clinging to the tail of an aircraft of one of the other *Staffeln*. A quick rocking motion to alert my wingman, and we dived down at full speed to attack him from behind.

'I opened fire at 50 metres, letting fly with everything I had. The enemy machine side-slipped to port, desperately trying to escape, but I stuck with him. I could clearly see my shots striking his tail. All at once he flipped over on to his back like a dying fish, then started to go down in ever steepening spirals, before finally diving vertically into the ground.'

As aerial opposition dwindled, the pilots of I.(Z)/LG 1 were put to other tasks. Leutnant Methfessel found himself train-busting one day along the stretch of line between Bialystok and Warsaw. After shooting up two goods trains;

'I continued to fly at low level. But the rails remained obstinately empty. It didn't seem as if any more trains were coming.

'Then I saw an aircraft ahead of me – flying at an altitude of about 100 metres and following the line of the railway just as I was. It was a Ju 87. I could identify it by the wings, the short fixed undercarriage and the shape of the tail. "So", I thought, "he's the one who's been scaring all the trains away. But now it's my turn. And I'm faster than he is".

'I shot past some five metres underneath him. A quick glance upwards . . . and my blood froze – a large radial engine? And, as if I needed any more convincing, red-and-white checkerboards beneath each wing. He was a Pole. A Polish PZL P.23 light bomber.

'Under normal circumstances he would have posed no problem. But here I was presenting myself to him on a plate, completely helpless. Impossible to throttle back in the split-second left to me. Any moment now I would emerge from under his nose – a gift for his machine guns.

'There was only one thing to do. Expecting to feel his bullets striking home at any moment, I broke away in a gentle turn to starboard, seeking the safety of the earth like a crow with a hawk on its tail. And all the time the same cold feeling: he's going to start shooting – now!

'But he didn't. Scraping the tops of some conifers, I took a few deep breaths. The Pole continued to fly along the railway line, turning neither right nor left, as if he himself were on rails.

'Suddenly my wireless-operator opened up with his machine-gun. "Are you crazy?", I yelled, for we weren't out of trouble yet. But still nothing happened. The Pole was still flying a perfectly straight course – you could almost begin to believe it was a ghost plane, not piloted by human hands.

'Easing off on the throttles, I curved back in behind him. Now I was the hunter and he the hunted. Closing to within 50 metres, I opened fire. Two short bursts, five rounds from each cannon, and he went down in a fireball in front of me. A fine spray of hot oil filmed my windscreen. And then I saw him hit the ground and disintegrate right on top of the railway embankment.'

By the third week of September the Polish retreat had become a rout. The remnants of the Polish army were streaming back towards Warsaw. The Luftwaffe was ordered to attack this fleeing mass without let-up. From dawn to dusk hundreds of aircraft were sent in to bomb and strafe the columns choking the roads, lanes and woodland paths leading to the River Vistula.

I.(Z)/LG 1 were not spared this unpalatable duty. Called down from East Prussia, they were allotted a strip of territory some 35 km long, from the confluence of the Bzura and Vistula rivers due west to the small township of Gabin, and given ten minutes – five minutes one way, and five minutes back – to use up all their ammunition.

After it was all over they headed back to base. Last to land were Major Grabmann and the *Stabsschwarm*. As the *Kommandeur* clambered out of the cockpit and stood on the port wing of his aircraft, the three *Staffelkapitäne* stepped forward to report.

'Thank you, *meine Herren*', Major Grabmann said as he slowly climbed down to the ground, 'I don't think that was easy for any of us. Personally, I would prefer a good, clean dogfight any day'.

THE 'PHONEY WAR'

The end of the campaign in Poland was followed by nearly eight months of virtual inactivity in the west as the opposing ground forces – German on the one hand, Anglo-French on the other – settled in behind their respective fortifications, each waiting for the other to make the first move. With little more than local patrolling going on, it was a period which came to be known as the 'Phoney War'.

It was a different story in the air above the strip of no-man's land separating the *Westwall* from the Maginot Line, however. Weather permitting, both sides sent up reconnaissance machines to test and probe the others' defences, while maintaining standing fighter patrols to protect the integrity of their own. The Luftwaffe relied exclusively on the Bf 109-equipped *Jagdgruppen* to defend its western airspace. This fact, coupled with the total lack of large-scale offensive activity on the part of the *Kampfgeschwader*, meant that the *Zerstörers'* long-range patrol and escort services were temporarily surplus to requirements along the Western Front.

The coming months would not be wasted, however. It was a time of reinforcement and rapid expansion as the Luftwaffe sought to bolster its strength along the Rhine. All three of the *Zerstörergruppen* which had been engaged over Poland were quickly transferred westwards. And although no new *Zerstörer* units were activated, the opportunity was taken finally to re-equip the seven original *Gruppen* still flying the Bf 109 with their long-awaited twin-engined Bf 110s.

Major Grabmann's I.(Z)/LG 1 left Poland in October to take up residence at Würzburg, in central Germany. At the same time, a reorganisation of their parent *Lehrgeschwader* resulted in their redesignation as V.(Z)/LG 1. The most successful *Zerstörergruppe* in Poland now became the first to take the Bf 110 into combat in the west. On at least two of the

Having begun the war flying Bf 109Ds under the temporary designation of *Jagdgruppe* 152, Hauptmann Lessmann's I./ZG 52 converted to the Bf 110C early in 1940. Here, they are seen familiarising themselves with their new twin-engined machines; flying an impeccable *Schwarm* formation over the Austrian Alps

very few incursions made by Bf 110s into French airspace before the end of 1939, the *Gruppe* clashed with fighters of the *Armée de l'Air*. Escorting a reconnaissance Dornier over the Reims region on 21 November, one *Staffel* had an inconclusive brush with defending Curtiss Hawk H-75As and Morane MS.406s. Forty-eight hours later, Leutnant Werner Methfessel, who had taken over as acting *Staffelkapitän* of 3.(Z)/LG 1 (now 15.(Z)/LG 1) after Hauptmann Schleif had been brought down by anti-aircraft fire near Deblin on 7 September, claimed an MS.406 over Verdun.

Some doubt surrounds the veracity of the latter claim, for the only known French loss on 23 November was a Curtiss Hawk shot down by a Do 17. This could conceivably be yet another case of mis-identification (albeit by both sides!) and, if so, Methfessel's victory was not only the first to be achieved by a Bf 110 pilot in the west, it also took his personal score to five, thus making him the Luftwaffe's very first *Zerstörer* ace.

Although the bulk of the *Zerstörerwaffe* – once re-equipped with the Bf 110 – would find little to do along the Franco-German border, there was one area where the twin-engined fighter's presence was to prove decisive.

Within minutes of Prime Minister Neville Chamberlain's declaration of war against Germany at 1100 on the morning of 3 September 1939, RAF Bomber Command had begun 'trailing its coat' along the Reich's North Sea shores. The increasing tenor of British reconnaissance and bombing raids, and the protests of the Kriegsmarine – whose ships, whether in dock or at sea, were the primary target of all these early forays – resulted in a strengthening of the region's aerial defences. A *Geschwaderstab* was set up to coordinate the miscellany of fighter *Gruppen* drafted in to the area. Identified by a variety of official designations,

19

the collection of units became more commonly known as the *Jagdgeschwader* 'Schumacher' after its *Kommodore*.

Schumacher's original force, made up entirely of early mark Bf 109s, had already proved capable of inflicting damage on the RAF bomber formations. But what was really needed was a longer-range machine able to intercept the raiders far out to sea, which could then continue to harry them during their bombing runs and, if necessary, chase them back out over open water. The Luftwaffe had just such an aircraft in the shape of the Bf 110.

It was hardly surprising, therefore, that the first of the seven Bf 109-equipped *Zerstörergruppen* to begin conversion on to the twin-engined Bf 110 was one currently serving under the *Jagdgeschwader* 'Schumacher' – Hauptmann Kaschka's I./ZG 26, based at Varel, south of Wilhelmshaven.

I./ZG 26 were in the middle of their re-equipment programme when, on 3 December 1939, offshore radar reported enemy bombers approaching Heligoland. The *Gruppe* scrambled a formation each of Bf 109Ds and Bf 110Cs. The latter, however, failed to make an interception. Three days later I./ZG 26 scored its first success with the Bf 110, but unfortunately suffered its first loss at one and the same time, when a 2. *Staffel* machine was involved in a mid-air collision with a Coastal Command Anson off the Dutch island of Texel.

Somebody must have realised the folly of attempting to convert on to an entirely new type of aircraft (complete with an additional engine and crew member!) while remaining on operations, for on 7 December 1. and 3./ZG 26 decamped inland to re-equip in relative peace. This left just the Bf 110s of 2. *Staffel* on the coast to bridge the gap until the arrival of a more experienced *Zerstörer* unit. The replacements were to be those veterans of the Polish campaign, Hauptmann Reinecke's I./ZG 76, who began to move in to Jever on 16/17 December. They could not have arrived at a more opportune moment.

The morning of 18 December dawned fine and clear. The sky was a vault of the palest blue, a perfect winter's day, with perfect visibility – and perfect fighter weather. Yet, on this date, Bomber Command despatched a force of 24 Wellingtons to mount yet another assault on Germany's North Sea coastline. Buoyed by a false sense of optimism (a recent drubbing at the hands of a *Gruppe* of Bf 109Es had been dismissed, the losses being ascribed to naval flak!), and still convinced, despite mounting evidence to the contrary, that a disciplined formation of bombers 'would always get through', RAF planners had selected Wilhelmshaven as the day's target. The resulting mayhem has since gone down in history as the 'Battle of the German Bight'.

The crews of I./ZG 76 had spent the morning on a series of patrols in *Schwarm* and *Rotte* strength, familiarising themselves with their new area of operations. They were up again early in the afternoon when reports began to filter in announcing the approach of British bombers. Communications problems between the coastal radar sites and the airfields, coupled with frank disbelief by some unit commanders, delayed the Luftwaffe's response. Twenty-two Wellingtons (two having aborted) paraded across Wilhelmshaven in faultless array, unhindered by anything other than the Kriegsmarine's ship- and shore-based flak.

It was not until the bombers had turned for home, having split up and now heading west parallel to the coast in two separate formations approximately 15 km and 40 km out to sea respectively, that Schumacher's fighters finally caught up with them – over an hour after the original radar sighting! First to pounce were some half-dozen Bf 109s, but it was the *Zerstörer* of I./ZG 76, once they had made contact, who had the longer legs to chase the fleeing bombers westwards along the chain of German and Dutch Frisian Islands, and who would subsequently claim the lion's share of the kills.

Some Bf 110s were already aloft. The indefatigable Wolfgang Falck, *Staffelkapitän* of 2./ZG 76, and his wingman Unteroffizier Heinz Fresia, for example, were patrolling off Borkum, westernmost of the German Frisian Islands, when they heard the reports of enemy bombers passing Heligoland. Quickly reversing course, they headed north-eastwards, climbing steadily. The bursts of flak staining the sky over Wilhelmshaven far off to starboard were clearly visible. Moments later they could also make out the distant specks of 12 or more Wellingtons, still under attack by the last of the Bf 109s, dead ahead.

As soon as they were within range, the two Bf 110s joined the fray. Falck selected the right-hand aircraft of the rear section of bombers, which broke up in mid-air under the combined onslaught of his cannon and machine-guns, whilst a second reportedly crashed after he disabled one of its engines. Heinz Fresia also sent two of the Wellingtons down into the sea in flames, but not before his leader's aircraft had been hit by return fire from one of the bombers. With one engine dead and the other faltering, and with fuel pouring out of the wing, Falck limped south to force-land on the island of Wangerooge, which he later wryly described as, 'An experience that cured me for life of ever wanting to become a glider pilot!'

Other pilots of I./ZG 76 were caught on the ground. Leutnant Helmut Lent had just landed after a two-hour patrol;

'Punctually, at 1230 hours, the *Kommandeur* had started to roll, and our two *Schwärme* had lifted off in perfect formation. We climbed up to 4000 metres. For us, only just arrived on the coast, the sea presented a marvellous picture. Hardly a cloud in the sky. As far as the eye could see, the majestic tranquillity of a beautiful midwinter's day.

'After two hours we headed back to base, somewhat disappointed that the patrol had been uneventful. The groundcrews immediately began to refuel the machines.

'As I climbed out of my aircraft to report my *Rotte*'s return to the *Kommandeur*, the chief mechanic came rushing up to me, shouting "Fifty *Engländer* had been sighted west of Heligoland". The fighters and some of our *Zerstörer* were already in action against them. I immediately informed the *Kommandeur*. As I did so, we all became aware of puffs of flak in the sky away to the east and the distant sound of guns. Then we caught sight of some of the fine gentlemen from England. About ten tiny dots being chased out to sea by the cotton-wool balls of anti-aircraft fire.

'"Whoever's ready to go, get after them", the *Kommandeur* yelled. My machine was the first to finish refuelling. I hurriedly scrambled back into the cockpit – my wireless-operator was already aboard. Switch on, full throttle, and we were off. My good old "Dora" climbed like a bird. After

Hauptmann Wolfgang Falck, *Staffelkapitän* of 2./ZG 76, pictured in snowy surroundings at the time of the 'Battle of the German Bight'. The inflatable life-jacket is indicative of the long overwater patrols the *Staffel* was flying during the winter of 1939-40

21

An example of how the contemporary German newspapers recorded the 18 December 'Battle'. A smiling Leutnant Helmut Lent in front of the tailfin of his aircraft. One of the last three victories indicated here (claimed over the Bight on that day) would subsequently be disallowed

Also from a newspaper of the time, two of the RAF survivors – below, a bandaged Flg Off P A Wimberley, the pilot of Lent's first victim, a No 37 Sqn Wellington IA which crash-landed on the island of Borkum. And on the right, flanked by two guards, a more cheerful Sgt H Ruse. Again from No 37 Sqn, he managed to bring his crippled Wellington down on the *Watt*, or mud flats, off the island of Spiekeroog

only a few minutes we had reached the same altitude as the "Tommies". The chase was on.

'Almost as if to order, a pair of "Britishers" drifted into my gunsights. They were slightly separated from the rest of their squadron. The first thing to do was to silence their rear turrets. This was accomplished by a few short, well-aimed, bursts of fire. Now I could move in for the kill. At close range, and at an altitude of only some 2000 metres – so much height had we lost already – I sent a few more rounds into one of the enemy bombers. Thick smoke poured out of it. The English pilot did what he could, trying to land on a German island. But his aircraft was already a mass of flames.

'One down. And now for the second "Tommy". He was trying to get away at low level – only some 4-5 metres above the wavetops. I chased after him at maximum speed. No sign of life from the rear gunner. Once more I closed right in before letting loose with everything I had. A bright tongue of flame shot out of his wing. The enemy aircraft reared up briefly and then plunged into the sea. A thick column of smoke climbed into the sky from the circle of burning fuel and oil marking the spot where he had broken up.

'My wireless-operator and I scoured the horizon for fresh opponents. Success! Some distance away, further out to sea, we saw a few more "Tommies" already under attack from two of our comrades. With "full speed", I set off in pursuit. Soon I was on the tail of another enemy bomber which, at that moment, was not being engaged. Although I closed right up to him, there was again no return fire from the rear turret. In the tried and tested manner, I let him have all barrels at minimum range, and this time succeeded in setting both his wing tanks ablaze. The pilot obviously attempted an emergency landing on the water, but the bomber went in nose first and immediately sank like a stone.'

As recounted at the start of this chapter, Lent flew back to Jever convinced he had scored a triple success. However, after closer investigation, nearly a third of the 38 kills claimed by the *Jagdgeschwader* 'Schumacher' that day were subsequently disallowed by the authorities. This included three out of I./ZG 76's total of 16 – Falck's second, one of Lent's and the single claim submitted by future ace Gordon Gollob. Bomber Command's actual losses were 11 Wellingtons shot down during the course of the 30-minute running fight, and six so badly damaged that they later crashed or crash-landed.

After its success in the offensive against Poland, this latest demonstration of the Bf 110's equal prowess as a defensive bomber-destroyer must have been music indeed to the ears of Generalfeldmarschall Hermann Göring. In an after-action report on the 18 December, 'Battle' *Gruppenkommandeur* Hauptmann Reinecke wrote;

'The Bf 110 is capable of catching and destroying this English type (i.e. Vickers Wellington) quite easily, even at low speeds, where attacks can be carried out in quick succession, from both sides as well as from the front quarters. Such frontal quarter attacks can be particularly effective when the enemy machine flies into the cone of fire. The Wellington burns easily and is generally very prone to catching light.'

Although the RAF had finally got the message, transferring its allegiance from the unescorted daylight bomber to the cloak of night for the forthcoming offensive against Germany proper, Bomber Command was still being ordered to send aircraft on 'armed reconnaissance sweeps' of the North Sea. The first of these to be mounted since the fateful 18 December encounter was carried out by 17 Wellingtons on 2 January 1940. One trio of bombers was bounced by a *Schwarm* of I./ZG 76's Bf 110s with predictable consequences – only one Wellington made it back to base.

Eight days later the *Gruppe* brought down a Blenheim near Heligoland, and on 17 February another was shot into the sea north of the Dutch island of Ameland. This latter kill was credited to Hauptmann Falck. Two other intervening claims being unsubstantiated, this finally brought his proven score of enemy aircraft destroyed to five, thus making Wolfgang Falck a serious challenger for the title of the Luftwaffe's first Bf 110 *Zerstörer* ace.

SCANDINAVIA

Falck's undoubted talents as a pilot and combat leader were rewarded by his promotion to the command of I./ZG 1 prior to the Wehrmacht's next offensive venture. The occupation and invasion of Denmark and Norway, which would re-unite two of the three veteran *Zerstörergruppen* from the Polish campaign, offered yet again those essential prerequisites for successful Bf 110 operations – long distances and piecemeal opposition.

The two units had clearly defined roles. I./ZG 1 would occupy the Danish airfields, and here they would remain, their presence serving both to extend the Luftwaffe's 'defensive belt' around the German Bight and to

Bf 110 UNITS IN THE SCANDINAVIAN CAMPAIGN

X. Fliegerkorps HQ: Hamburg

		Base	Type	Est-Serv
I./ZG 76	Hpt Günther Reinecke	Westerland	Bf 110C	32-29
3./ZG 1	Oblt Walter Ehle	Westerland	Bf 110C	10-9
1.&2./ZG 1	Hpt Wolfgang Falck	Barth	Bf 110C	22-17

secure the aerial transport corridors across the Skagerrak to Oslo and Stavanger, in Norway. After participating in the opening stages in Denmark, I./ZG 76 alone would move up into Norway to continue the fight northwards.

I./ZG 1's lot was by far the easier of the two. Shortly after 0700 hours on 9 April 1940, elements of the *Gruppe* took off from their base at Barth, on the Baltic coast, to escort He 111 bombers of KG 4 in 'shows of strength' over key areas in Denmark, including the capital Copen-

A rather unconvincing propaganda photograph of a groundcrewman 'painting' his pilot's latest victory on the tailfin of his aircraft. But the scoreboard merits closer inspection – three Polish, four British and one Danish! This combination can only be that claimed by Wolfgang Falck, the last kill bar indicating the D.XXI brought down over Vaerlöse – see profile four in the colour section

hagen. At Vaerlöse airfield, a Danish Fokker D.XXI attempting to take off was immediately despatched by Hauptmann Falck. Four other D.XXIs and ten Fokker C-VEs dispersed about the field were then destroyed by ground-strafing.

But perhaps the most memorable event of that opening morning was Oberleutnant Victor Mölders' single-handed occupation of the Danish town of Aalborg. This was a task officially assigned to a company of paratroopers, who had already been dropped on the two nearby airfields. 1./ZG 1 followed them in, and soon after landing, *Staffelkapitän* Oberleutnant Martin Lutz ordered Mölders (brother of the legendary Werner) to go into town and secure suitable quarters for the aircrew. Still dressed in full flying gear, Mölders asked exactly how he was supposed to get there. Lutz gently took him by the arm and pointed beyond the perimeter fence. 'Look', he said, 'there is the road. Cars drive along it. Hitch a lift'.

So Mölders did just that. Trudging to the wire, he was soon picked up by an obliging Danish milking machine salesman. On the way into Aalborg the car passed columns of paras doggedly marching along on either side of the road. Suggesting to Mölders that they drop in at his house for a bite of breakfast, the salesman took the opportunity to reassure his wife that, despite the announcements issuing from the radio, the 'invasion was nothing for her to worry about'. He then drove the bemused Oberleutnant the rest of the way, depositing him in front of a rather luxurious hotel. It was not until the necessary formalities had been completed that it suddenly dawned on Victor Mölders — he was the first, and as yet still the only, member of the German armed forces in town!

I./ZG 1 would be based at Aalborg for close on a month. Although they saw little action during this period, the growing number of RAF bombers overflying the region by night prompted the ever-resourceful Falck to take matters into his own hands again. At these latitudes, the raiders were often visible silhouetted against the slightly lighter northern sky. Falck therefore selected five of his most experienced crews and, with himself at their head, set up what he somewhat grandiosely entitled his '*Dämmerungsbereitschaftsflotte*' (literally 'dusk readiness fleet') and started experimenting with a primitive form of nightfighting.

Falck's "fleet" even managed to intercept and engage three RAF bombers at night, but all escaped into the darkness nearer the ground.

These unofficial trials had to be abandoned shortly thereafter, for the whole *Gruppe* was transferred down to the Ruhr at the beginning of May in readiness for the forthcoming assault on France and the Low Countries.

Hauptmann Reinecke's I./ZG 76 undoubtedly bore the brunt of *Zerstörer* operations in Scandinavia. Like I./ZG 1, their first job would be to escort paratroop-laden Ju 52s to two enemy airfields and suppress the defences prior to the actual paradrops. Unlike I./ZG 1, however, their two objectives were in Norway. The Bf 110s would have insufficient fuel to make the return flight across the Skagerrak, and so had been ordered to land on the target airfields as soon as these had been secured by the paratroops.

On the morning of 9 April two *Staffeln* of Bf 110s duly lifted off from Westerland, on the island of Sylt, to rendezvous with their tri-motored charges. 3./ZG 76, led by Oberleutnant Gollob, was to support the occupation of Stavanger-Sola, while Oberleutnant Werner Hansen's 1./ZG 76 headed for the Norwegian capital, Oslo-Fornebu (the *Gruppenstab* and 2. *Staffel* moved into newly-occupied Aalborg to provide back-up).

But thick fog and heavy cloud over the Skagerrak caused utter confusion. Separated from his *Staffel* in the deepening murk, Gollob ordered them to turn back for Denmark. Only the first *Schwarm* acknowledged, leaving the remaining two *Rotten* to plough on until one pair collided in mid-air – wreckage was subsequently recovered from the sea. The remaining two completed the mission, arriving over Stavanger-Sola moments before the paratroops dropped, and putting down on the field some 30 minutes later with their fuel almost exhausted.

The eight Bf 110s of 1. *Staffel* en route to Oslo-Fornebu also suffered mixed fortunes. Plunging through the gloom, they were unaware that the first wave of Ju 52s carrying the paratroops had already turned back, and when a signal from *Fliegerkorps* HQ ordered them to do the same, it was too late. The *Zerstörer* were already past the point of no return, and would have to land somewhere on the far side of the Skagerrak come what may.

Suddenly they burst through into bright sunlight over Oslo Fjord, only to be set upon by seven Norwegian Gladiators. In the dogfight which ensued, each side lost two aircraft (one of the Gladiators providing Helmut Lent with his fifth confirmed victory), while a number of others were damaged.

Battling on to Oslo-Fornebu, the six surviving Bf 110s proceeded to strafe the airfield defences according to plan. Their fuel reserves had allowed them just 20 minutes for the task, and this time was long spent before the first of the Ju 52s finally hove into view. But instead of disgorging sticks of paratroopers, the transports formed into an unmistakable landing pattern. They were part of the second wave bringing in the airborne infantry to consolidate the non-existent drop zone!

As the leading transports touched down they came under heavy fire. Several managed to open up and take-off again, but with many of those following still determined to land, others veering away intent on returning to Denmark and the Bf 110s out of fuel, the situation was becoming critical. Hansen had few options left. He ordered Lent to attempt a landing while he and the other four Bf 110s gave covering fire.

With his starboard engine already damaged in the clash with the

In this shot it can be seen just how close Lent came to hitting the trees and house bordering the landing strip. Undeterred by events below, a Ju 52 passes low overhead as it comes in to land, bringing in more airborne infantry. Note the score-board above the swastika on Lent's machine, and what appears to be a wraparound 'flash' adorning the tail-cone – the latter perhaps a marking to assist formating in the air?

Gladiators, Lent came in fast. Narrowly missing a landing Ju 52 at the intersection of the field's two runways, he braked as hard as he dared but was unable to stop the Bf 110 from careering off the end of the tarmac, smashing through the perimeter wire and down a boundary slope. With its undercarriage sheared off, the machine finally came to rest nuzzling a picket fence surrounding a stand of trees in the garden of a house along-side the airfield.

Conditions at Stavanger-Sola seem to have been little better than those at Oslo-Fornebu. Here, both 'M8+CK' of 2./ZG 76 and an unidentified He 111 bomber have nosed over in the soft ground upon landing

Two more *Zerstörer* (including the aircraft flown by Werner Hansen) managed to get down safely despite earlier damage inflicted by the Gladiators. The other three landed virtually unscathed. The *Staffelkapitän* quickly deployed his small force of mobile Bf 110s around the airfield in positions offering the five rear-gunners the most advantageous fields of fire, but Oslo-Fornebu's defenders had already been given orders to withdraw. The way was clear for the remaining Ju 52s to land.

The day's alarms were not over yet for 1./ZG 76, however. Presumably having pulled rank to commandeer two of the undamaged Bf 110s, Hansen and Lent were patrolling Oslo Fjord in the early hours of the evening when they chanced upon an inquisitive RAF Sunderland, which the former promptly shot down.

Within hours the Wehrmacht's grip on southern Norway was secure. By 11 April the whole of I./ZG 76 was concentrated at Stavanger, ready to support the ground forces' push northwards, and to protect the country's western seaboard, with its vital inshore shipping lanes, from attack by the RAF from across the North Sea. This set the pattern for the coming weeks.

The Bf 110s were aided in their endeavours by some half-dozen Ju 88s. Immediately prior to the Norwegian campaign, one of the bomber units involved (the Ju 88-equipped KG 30) had established its own semi-autonomous *Zerstörerstaffel* for the specific purpose of providing long-range escort and patrol capabilities. Flying Ju 88C-2s (the first fighter variant of the prolific Ju 88 family to be built), pilots of Z/KG 30 were to claim a number of RAF aircraft over Norway. Although none is believed to have gained ace status at this time, at least two – Leutnant Manfred Riegel and Unteroffizier Peter Lauffs – did so later after the *Staffel* was incorporated into the nightfighter arm (see *Osprey Aircraft of the Aces 20 - German Nightfighter Aces of World War 2* for details).

Throughout April I./ZG 76's scoreboard grew, 'fed' by a 'steady diet' of RAF Wellingtons, Blenheims and Hudsons. By the latter half of the month, action was focussed around central Norway – scene of Anglo-French landings on 18 and 19 April. Here, the *Gruppe* encountered Gladiators again, but this time RAF examples flown in aboard the carrier HMS

Furious, and operating from a makeshift airstrip on the frozen surface of Lake Lesjakog, where many were to be destroyed by bombing and ground-strafing.

On the last day of April the *Gruppe* suffered their hardest blow of the campaign when not only *Kommandeur* Günther Reinecke, but also two of 3. *Staffel*'s most successful pilots in Leutnant Helmut Fahlbusch and Oberfeldwebel Georg Fleischmann, with six and five victories respectively, were killed in action against British bombers. Werner Hansen took over as acting *Kommandeur* until the arrival of Reinecke's replacement, Hauptmann Werner Restemeyer, on 11 May.

By this time, all Anglo-French forces had been evacuated from central Norway, and operations were now concentrated in the far north of the country around the last remaining Allied enclaves at Narvik, well above the Arctic Circle. The immense distances involved in this final stage of the campaign proved too much even for the *Zerstörer*, but this problem had been foreseen, and feverish efforts had been made to develop an auxiliary fuel tank which would increase the Bf 110's range. The end result took the form of a 1050-litre ventral tank, enclosed in a large streamlined wooden fairing.

The first of these Bf 110Ds, as the converted aircraft were officially designated, were delivered to I./ZG 76 at Stavanger-Forbus. A special *Staffel* was organised, commanded by *Gruppen*-Adjutant Oberleutnant Hans Jäger, and made up of the most experienced crews from all three of the other *Staffeln*. This unit was then transferred to Trondheim on 18 May. Although the Bf 110D allowed Jäger's eight-strong *Staffel* to carry out lengthy overwater patrols, and to also undertake bomber-escort missions on the four-and-a-half-hour, 1300-km, round trip between Trondheim and Narvik, it was heartily disliked by most of those who flew it.

The enormous size of the Bf 110D's ventral fuel tank is well illustrated in this frontal view. This photograph serves to show how drastically the Bf 110's otherwise relatively clean lines were altered by the ventral fairing. It is hardly surprising that combat reports penned by RAF pilots meeting these monstrosities described them as 'Dornier bombers'!

The seemingly ever-cheerful Helmut Lent pictured much later in his career as a highly successful night-fighter pilot. Among his many awards and decorations, the *Narvikschild* (Narvik Shield) on his left sleeve bears witness to his service with ZG 76 over Norway in the spring of 1940. Members of all three armed services of the Wehrmacht who fought in and around Narvik were eligible for the shield

Dubbed the '*Dackelbauch*' ('Dachshund belly') for obvious reasons, the D-model's handling characteristics left a lot to be desired, particularly when there was unused fuel sloshing about in the bottom of the cavernous ventral tank. This latter, it was claimed, also filled the cockpit with petrol fumes, and was a distinct fire hazard, whether empty or full.

The special *Staffel* nevertheless gave a good account of themselves against renewed RAF opposition, which comprised both Gladiator IIs of No 263 Sqn (after its costly attempt to operate from Lake Lesjakog, the unit had returned to Norway with a fresh complement of aircraft, flying in to Bardufoss, north of Narvik, from *Furious* on 20 May) and No 46 Sqn Hurricane Is – see *Osprey Aircraft of the Aces 18 - Hurricane Aces 1939-40* for details. The latter had arrived via the carrier HMS *Glorious*, joining the Gladiators at Bardufoss shortly after the biplane fighters had flown in.

On 27 May Helmut Lent shot down a No 263 Sqn Gladiator over Bødo, wounding its pilot, future Rhodesian RAF ace Flt Lt Caesar Hull. Forty-eight hours later *Staffelführer* Hans Jäger fell victim to a Hurricane west of Skaanland. He too survived, along with his gunner, but both became prisoners-of-war.

In another engagement during this period Leutnant Reinhold Eckardt's wingman, Oberfeldwebel Neureiter, took a hit in one of his engines. Eckardt determined to shepherd the ailing Bf 110 the 650 km back to Trondheim. By judicial use of his throttles, and by flying on a single engine himself, using first one and then the other, he was able to hold his own speed down to that of his stricken wingman. And when Neureiter could no longer keep the Bf 110 in the air, but had to put it down on a frozen lake high in the mountains of central Norway, Eckardt circled above carefully marking the exact position on his map. He then set off for base, where both crews had long been given up for lost. A future night-fighter ace and Knight's Cross recipient, Eckardt finally landed back at Trondheim six and forty minutes after take-off!

The evacuation of the Allied expeditionary force from Narvik at the beginning of June brought an end to the special *Staffel*'s marathon round-flights. However, I./ZG 76 retained a presence at Trondheim for local defence duties, for although the whole of Norway was now in German hands, the British were still keeping up their air attacks on German shipping in Norwegian waters and on Luftwaffe-occupied airfields along the coast. One ambitious operation on 13 June attempted to combine the two – RAF bombers raiding Trondheim-Vaernes airfield as a prelude to a Fleet Air Arm dive-bombing attack on the damaged battle-cruiser *Scharnhorst* in harbour nearby.

In the event, everything went wrong. A depleted force of Beaufort bombers did little damage at Trondheim, serving merely to stir up the defending fighters (Bf 109s of II./JG 77 and Bf 110s of I./ZG 76), who promptly scrambled to give chase. The Beauforts could not be caught, but the Luftwaffe pilots lost all interest in the fleeing 'twins' when presented with the spectacle of a dozen or more unescorted Skua dive-bombers lumbering up Trondheim Fjord towards them.

The Skuas, each encumbered with a single 500-lb semi-armour piercing bomb intended for the *Scharnhorst*, were no match for the Messerschmitts. Eight were shot down in little more than as many minutes. Of the four claimed by 3./ZG 76, the first went to *Staffelkapitän* Gollob and the last to Oberfeldwebel Herbert Schob. Already a six-victory veteran of the *Condor Legion*, Schob had scored at least twice in Poland with I.(Z)/LG 1, and would survive the war as one of the most successful *Zerstörer* pilots of them all.

Despite some spectacular successes by the Skua earlier in the campaign, including the sinking of the cruiser *Königsberg*, the slaughter over Trondheim on 13 June 1940 marked the end of the dive-bomber as far as the British Admiralty was concerned. For the remainder of the war, once the last of the Skuas had been withdrawn from first-line service, Royal Navy carriers would embark only fighters and torpedo-bombers. Thus, six months almost to the day after I./ZG 76's participation in the 'Battle of the German Bight' had fundamentally altered Bomber Command's further prosecution of *its* war, this same *Gruppe* of Bf 110s had also been instrumental in imposing similar far-reaching changes on the Fleet Air Arm . . . quite a legacy for little more than two-dozen aircraft and crews!

Before the end of June, I./ZG 76 was concentrated back in Stavanger. From here they continued to bring down the occasional raider. On the morning of 9 July, again in the company of elements of II./JG 77, they inflicted another serious reversal on the RAF, reportedly shooting down half of a force of 12 attacking Blenheims. Four of these bombers were initially credited to Unteroffizier Fresia alone, but this number was later reduced to two (in all, defending Luftwaffe fighters had claimed 12 Blenheims destroyed, whilst actual British losses were seven). Later in the afternoon of 9 July, Oberleutnant Gollob intercepted a Sunderland far out over the North Sea. He chased it more than halfway back to the Shetlands before finally dispatching it. Later still, in the company of Herbert Schob, he also brought down a patrolling Hudson. Other Hudsons would fall victim to the *Gruppe* in the weeks ahead.

Total *Zerstörer* losses to all causes during the entire Norwegian campaign, and in the two months since, had numbered little more than 20. But by now the Battle of Britain was being fought in the skies of southern England. The relatively light casualties they had suffered to date ill prepared Hauptmann Werner Restemeyer, and his I./ZG 76, for the reception they were about to get in the one foray across the North Sea which was to be their sole contribution to that historic conflict.

Part of the all-Bf 110 *Zerstörerwaffe* which participated in the *Blitzkrieg* against France and the Low Countries, this machine of I./ZG 52 based at Neuhausen ob Eck displays the striking *Gruppe* badge of a white dragon on a black shield

Long before I./ZG 1 and I./ZG 76 had gone into Denmark and Norway, the six remaining Bf 109-equipped *Zerstörergruppen* had begun conversion on to the Bf 110. Most had started re-equipping back in February, and by the time of the invasion of France and the Low Countries on 10 May 1940, the *Zerstörerwaffe* was, at long last, an all-Bf 110 force.

But there were those who still harboured doubts as to the basic soundness of the long-range heavy fighter concept. In the weeks leading up to the assault on France, one of the recently re-equipped *Zerstörergruppen* found itself sharing an airfield with a unit of Bf 109s. Justifiably proud of their powerful new mounts, the *Zerstörer* pilots were dismissive of the nimble, but diminutive, single-seaters, and did little to disguise their good-natured disdain. Unfortunately for their collective peace of mind, the *Zerstörers'* co-occupants at Dortmund were JG 26. And while the majority of the Bf 109 pilots were content to turn a deaf ear to the jibes, there was one exception – JG 26's TO (Technical Officer), Walter Horten, who also happened to be one of the aircraft-designing Horten brothers.

Wing loadings, power-to-weight ratios and the like were 'meat and drink' to Walter Horten. Requesting permission to take one of the big Messerschmitts up on a test flight, Horten found his suspicions concerning the Bf 110's inherent flaws fully confirmed. He then invited the

Bf 110 UNITS IN THE WEST, 17 MAY 1940

Luftflottenkommando 2 HQ: **Münster**

		Base	Est-Serv
Jagdfliegerführer 2 (Dortmund)			
Stab ZG 26	Obstlt Joachim-Friedrich Huth	Dortmund	3-3
I./ZG 26	Hpt Wilhelm Makrocki	Niedermendig	34-11
III./ZG 26	Hpt Johannes Schalk	Krefeld	37-30
I./ZG 1	Hpt Wolfgang Falck	Kirchhellen	35-22
II./ZG 1	Hpt Friedrich-Karl Dickoré	Gelsenkirchen-Buer	36-26

Luftflottenkommando 3 HQ: **Bad Orb**

Jagdfliegerführer 3 (Wiesbaden)			
Stab ZG 2	Obstlt Friedrich Vollbracht	Darmstadt-Griesheim	3-2
I./ZG 2	Hpt Hannes Gentzen	Darmstadt-Griesheim	32-22
1.Fliegerkorps (Cologne)			
Stab ZG 76	Maj Walter Grabmann	Cologne-Wahn	3-3
II./ZG 76	Maj Erich Groth	Cologne-Wahn	33-25
II./ZG 26	Maj Ralph von Rettberg	Kaarst/Neuss	35-25
V.Fliegerkorps (Gersthofen)			
I./ZG 52	Hpt Karl-Heinz Lessmann	Neuhausen ob Eck	35-23
V.(Z)/LG 1	Hpt Horst Liensberger	Mannheim-Sandhofen	33-27

Zerstörer CO to nominate his best pilot, and challenged him to a mock dogfight. The two squared up to each other 3000 metres above the airfield in full view of those watching below. The Bf 110 was being flown by an experienced NCO ex-flying instructor, there was nobody in the back seat and it was carrying only half its normal load – his aircraft may have been brand new, but the *Zerstörer* CO hadn't been born yesterday . . . in fact, he was a one-legged veteran of World War 1!

Despite these precautions, Horten's Bf 109 was on its tail in a trice. They broke apart and began again – with exactly the same result. The Bf 110 pilot and his colleagues on the ground had to concede defeat. Horten did not rub salt into their wounded pride, but offered instead some friendly, and prophetic, advice;

'*Meine Herren,* be very careful if you should ever come up against the *Engländer.* Their fighters are all single-engined. And once they get to know the Bf 110's weaknesses, you could be in for a very nasty surprise!'

Initially, however, the Bf 110s would continue to give as good as they got in their new western theatre of operations. As the severe winter of 1939-40 gradually loosened its grip, encounters between *Zerstörer* and Anglo-French fighters had become more frequent. V.(Z)/LG 1 had one Bf 110 damaged and lost another in two separate clashes with RAF Hurricanes late in March. Then, on 2 April, Oberleutnant Methfessel put the question of his 'acedom' beyond any doubt by shooting down a French Morane MS.406 near Lunéville (his fifth, or sixth, kill of the war, depending upon the validity of his 23 November 1939 claim).

Five days after Methfessel's victory, the recently re-equipped I./ZG 2 lost two of their new Bf 110s to *Armée de l'Air* Curtiss Hawk 75As over the Argonne. Only one of the four crew members survived, albeit wounded and in temporary French captivity. But after his release following the capitulation of France in June, Leutnant Johannes Kiel would rise high in the ranks of the *Zerstörerwaffe.* This same engagement also provided *Gruppenkommandeur* Hauptmann Hannes Gentzen with his first kill on the Bf 110. Already the most successful pilot of the Polish campaign, this latest victory brought Gentzen's total of enemy aircraft destroyed to nine, which meant that for the next 16 days at least, a Bf 110 *Zerstörer* pilot topped the list as the highest scorer in the entire Luftwaffe

Equally as distinctive as I./ZG 52's *Gruppe* badge (seen on page 30) was I./ZG 2's blunderbuss-wielding 'Bernburger Jäger' ('Hunter of Bernburg') emblem, here painted beneath the cockpit of a taxying Bf 110. The most successful fighter *Gruppe* to emerge from the Polish campaign (where it had flown Bf 109s under the temporary guise of JGr 102 – see *Osprey Aircraft of the Aces 11 - Bf 109D/E Aces 1939-41* for details), I./ZG 2 had also utilised the 'Phoney War' period to re-equip with the twin-engined Bf 110

– his nearest rival, Hauptmann Werner Mölders of III./JG 53, would not claim his ninth until 23 April.

The opening rounds of the invasion of France and the Low Countries called upon the Bf 110s to repeat the tactics which had proved so successful in their two previous campaigns. On the southern and central sectors of the new front, the bulk of the *Zerstörergruppen* flew long-range escort missions aimed at crippling enemy air power exactly as they had done in Poland. In France alone, the Luftwaffe struck at nearly 50 Allied airfields. Taken by surprise, the defenders offered little in the way of resistance other than anti-aircraft fire, and even this was largely sporadic and inaccurate. Over Belgium, too, where II. and III./ZG 26 accompanied bombers attacking Charleroi and Antwerp, such raids were mainly uneventful.

Meanwhile, to the north over Holland, ZG 1 was carrying out ground-attack sorties to soften up Dutch airfield defences prior to paratroop and airborne landings in a re-run of the tactics employed against Denmark and Norway a month earlier. Hauptmann Falck's I. *Gruppe* were assigned to cover the airborne assaults of Rotterdam-Waalhaven and Hamstede, claiming 26 aircraft destroyed on the ground at the latter field. Where it could, the Dutch Air Force took to the air to offer opposition. A number of ZG 1 pilots claimed their first kills on this day, among them I. *Gruppe*'s NO (Communications Officer), Oberleutnant Werner Streib, who was later elevated to the very pinnacle of the nightfighter arm as *Inspekteur der Nachtjäger.*

But few can have been presented with so easy a victory as Leutnant Richard Marchfelder, Technical Officer of II./ZG 1, whose objective was Vlissingen (Flushing) airfield;

'Firstly, we strafed the machines lined up in rows in front of the hangars. Then we met a whole bunch of aircraft in the air apparently waiting for us. One of the *Holländer* tried to decoy us with some fancy aerobatics. First a loop, which brought him a bit closer to us, followed by an elegant roll. When he saw we weren't in the least bit impressed by these antics, he turned sharply to starboard. This put him bang in the middle of my sights. But before I could press the button he simply bailed out!'

The first day of fighting in the west ended with the loss of just two *Zerstörer*. This figure was multiplied threefold on 11 May, and included a brace of Bf 110s of I./ZG 2 shot down in action against RAF Hurricanes, despite their adopting a defensive circle. This manoeuvre, in which a unit under attack would form into a large circle where every crew – pilot and rear-gunner – could effectively cover the aircraft ahead and astern of them, had been developed by the original *Lehrgruppe* as the Bf 110's best means of defence. The 'defensive circle' was laid down in every *Zerstörer* pilot's handbook. Over the next three months the term would also appear with increasing frequency in RAF fighter pilots' after-action combat reports as embattled Bf 110s resorted to it more and more.

For the moment, though, the *Zerstörer* were still able, and more than willing, to 'mix it' with the uncoordinated Allied fighter opposition. On 12 May III./ZG 26 brought down eight enemy fighters over Belgium for no losses, one of the claimants being future ace Oberleutnant Sophus Baagoe. Two lean days followed, but 15 May was to prove one of the costliest of the campaign for the *Zerstörerwaffe*. Nine Bf 110s were lost

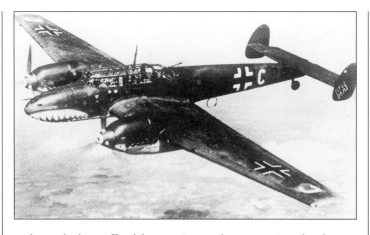

and several others suffered damage. Among the many actions that day was a fierce clash west of Laon between Hauptmann Heinz Nacke's 6./ZG 76 (part of the 'Sharksmouth' *Gruppe*) and Hurricanes of No 1 Sqn RAF. The latter's diarist recorded that 'These guys were good, confident and thirsting for a fight'. The results bear him out – Nacke lost two of his Bf 110s, but 6. *Staffel* shot down three of the Hurricanes.

The next day three Bf 110s went down. Again others were damaged, including that flown by Leutnant Wolfgang Schenck of 1./ZG 1, which was caught by nine Hurricanes near Brussels, resulting in the pilot being seriously wounded in the leg. After recovery, he rejoined his *Staffel*, by then operating as a fighter-bomber unit. Steadily climbing to the top of the ground-support command ladder, Schenck converted to the Me 262 jet bomber in 1944. He ended the war with 18 victories and as the *Inspizient für Strahlflugzeuge* (Inspector of Jet Aircraft) – see *Osprey Aircraft of the Aces 17 - German Jet Aces of World War 2*.

16 May was also the day another 'Sharksmouth' pilot scored his first victory, which proved to be the first of three kills on three consecutive days in fact. Oberfeldwebel Georg Anthony's experiences typify the *Zerstörer*'s war at this, the peak of their success. It all began when Anthony and five other Bf 110s of 4./ZG 76 were returning from an uneventful *freie Jagd* sweep of the Valenciennes-St Quentin-Le Cateau sectors. Cruising comfortably along at an altitude of about 500 metres, Anthony noticed a Henschel Hs 126 reconnaissance machine acting somewhat strangely;

'At first I thought "what's that Henschel doing fooling about down there". When I looked closer, I realised he was weaving about like mad dodging a *Franzmann* (Frenchman) who was trying to shoot him down.

'Naturally, we dived like the devil to get at the Frenchman. The *Staffelkapitän* and his wingman both built up too much speed and overshot. Then it was my turn. I let go a few brief bursts. At that very moment the Morane fell away to port and I lost sight of it for a few seconds.

'When I saw it again, it was heading south, racing low across the treetops of a small forest. We were after it like a shot. In a shallow dive, we quickly began to overhaul it. As we raced over enemy positions, the infantry threw themselves headlong to the ground as one man. During the chase I was firing without let-up, and the first hits were soon evident. The enemy machine was obviously trying to get back to base. In so doing,

A *Kette* of II./ZG 76 'Sharksmouths' revel in their mastery of the French skies as Allied forces are pushed back towards the Channel coast

it flew low across a forward airstrip. Again the same scene. As if cut down by a scythe, everybody fell flat on their faces in the dirt as the three aircraft roared low overhead – the Morane, and right on its tail two "Sharksmouths".

'The Frenchman was still in the air, even though his fuselage was shot full of holes. Shortly after passing over the forward landing field the enemy pilot lowered his flaps. I was on top of him in a second and had time for only a short burst before I had to pull up to avoid ramming him. I was still roughly level with the enemy machine when its fuel tank exploded.

'A bright sheet of flame. The machine hit the ground with an almighty crash and then flew back into the air as fresh explosions tore the fuselage to shreds. By now just one huge fireball, it cartwheeled three or four times into a cornfield.'

Another day, another mission. On 17 May two *Schwärme* of 4./ZG 76 escorted nine He 111s bombing a railway station near the town of Albert. It was not until the return flight that enemy fighters arrived on the scene. Ignoring the Heinkels, which were rapidly disappearing eastwards, a mixed formation of some 30 Moranes and Curtiss Hawks climbed towards the *Zerstörer*. Georg Anthony again;

'The enemy fighters approached, some from below, some from either side. The remarkable thing was – they must have been excellent pilots, by the way – they were performing the most extraordinary aerobatics. Presumably they thought this would make them a more difficult target for us to aim at.

'It was quite a sight. Our eight machines continuing steadily on their way, while all around the enemy were looping, banking, executing tight turns and barrel rolls. I can't remember now exactly when the shooting started. But I do recall my earphones being full of excited chatter.'

In the dogfight which ensued, Anthony got shots in at two Hawks, the second of which dived away trailing smoke . . .

'Then another enemy fighter came into my sight. This time it was a Morane, glued to the tail of another "Sharksmouth".

'"This one's mine", I thought to myself. I was in a perfect position. From short range I sent a few well-aimed rounds into his fat, rounded belly. The enemy single-seater reared up vertically for a moment, and then fell away on one wing. It went down vertically, slowly turning on its own axis, flames from both wings leaving a thick pall of smoke in its wake. I lost sight of it then as I got caught up in the dogfight again.'

Running low on fuel, the Bf 110s landed at Philippeville to refill their tanks. Here, Anthony's Morane was confirmed by other pilots, who had seen it hit the ground. Altogether, the *Zerstörer* claimed six of the French fighters without loss to themselves. Twenty-four hours later, Anthony was one of a *Schwarm* of just four Bf 110s escorting a formation of Do 17s sent in at low-level to attack troop columns near Cambrai. Again, it was not until the *Zerstörer* were returning to base that they were set upon – this time by a single French fighter. Anthony was the first to spot it;

'. . . about 200 metres above us. Another good old Morane. Suddenly, this daredevil dived out of the sun to attack our rearmost aircraft. Within moments he was on its tail, blazing away at a range of 100 metres.

'Our *Schwarmführer*, Oberleutnant Christiansen, immediately reefed into a 180° turn to confront him head-on. But the enemy stall-turned just as quickly to come at the leader from below.

'I went into a steep dive. For a moment the enemy crate was hidden by one of our own aircraft. But as I pulled out, it was sitting dead-centre in the illuminated ring of my gunsight. All I had to do was press the button. I kept my thumb down as I closed in. His port wing was suddenly enveloped in bright orange flames. The machine staggered and went into a climb – for a brief second the wing roundel shone in the light of the sun – then it tumbled earthwards, scattering its wreckage near the large Canadian World War 1 cemetery to the north-east of Cambrai.'

It is not just accounts such as these, describing the Bf 110 at the height of its powers, which are representative. Georg Anthony himself offers a perfect example of the fledgling *Zerstörer Experte* of this period, gaining confidence and kills in the opening stages of the campaign in the west, but facing ever growing opposition until finally cut down over southern England during the coming summer – Anthony, in fact, survived longer than many, finally being shot down and killed by Hurricanes from Nos 56 and 303 'Polish' Sqns over Hertfordshire on 30 August 1940.

Before that, however, the Battle of France had already taken its toll of existing aces. On the day of Anthony's second kill, 17 May, V.(Z)/LG 1 lost its highest scorer when Oberleutnant Werner Methfessel, *Kapitän* of 14. *Staffel*, fell victim again to RAF Hurricanes west of Reims.

18 May was another day of heavy losses for the *Zerstörerwaffe*; eight Bf 110s failing to return. Among them was the aircraft flown by Major Walter Grabmann, the *Condor Legion* veteran who had led I.(Z)/LG 1 so successfully in Poland, and who was now *Geschwaderkommodore* of ZG 76. Caught by RAF fighters near Dinant, Grabmann bailed out at low-level. After temporary captivity in French hands, he resumed command of ZG 76 for the Battle of Britain and beyond. He was promoted to the first of a succession of staff positions in 1941, having added six kills on the Bf 110 to those previously scored in Spain.

As German ground forces neared the Channel ports, the Luftwaffe faced increasing resistance from RAF fighters in the skies above. In a series of clashes over Boulogne and Calais on 23 May, elements of both ZGs 26 and 76 scored a number of kills, including the eighth to be claimed by Major Erich Groth, *Kommandeur* of II./ZG 76. Among their opponents, and providing at least one of their victims, were the Spitfires of No 92 Sqn, whose CO, Sqn Ldr R J Bushell, was last seen chasing a Bf 110 inland at low-level. Hit in the engine, Roger Bushell crash-landed east of Boulogne. After nearly four years as a PoW, Bushell, in his role as 'Big X' (head of the escape committee), organised and participated in 'The Great Escape' – the mass break-out from *Stalag Luft III* at Sagan by 76 prisoners in March 1944. Fifty of the recaptured escapees, including Bushell, were subsequently shot by the Gestapo.

Although no *Zerstörer* were lost on 23 May, three were damaged and five aircrew wounded, including Oberleutnant Günther Specht, *Gruppenadjutant* of I./ZG 26, and his wireless-operator/rear-gunner. Having already claimed the destruction of three RAF fighters over Calais, Specht's wounds, plus damage to his machine, then forced him to land between Calais and Boulogne (in the vicinity, perhaps, of Roger Bushell's Spitfire?).

Whilst the aircrews enjoyed the freedom of the skies over France and the low countries, things looked a little different from the ground-crews' perspective. As the *Zerstörergruppen* moved forward into occupied France in order to keep pace with the advancing armies, the amenities of home bases were left behind. Here, half-a-dozen men struggle with a recalcitrant tail-wheel on II./ZG 1's '2N+DM' (Wk-Nr 3026)

Specht had opened his scoreboard on 29 September 1939 by downing two Hampdens over the German Bight when I./ZG 26 was still flying the Bf 109D. He claimed a Wellington in the same area on 3 December, but received facial wounds from return fire which resulted in the loss of his left eye. Now wounded a second time, he would return to combat in single-seaters later in the war, only to be posted missing in the 1945 New Year's Day attack on Allied airfields.

The day after Specht's forced landing, another North Sea Bf 109D veteran was wounded. In fact, Oberleutnant Rolf Kaldrack had already scored three kills with the *Condor Legion* in Spain before claiming one of the Wellingtons downed in the 'Battle of the German Bight' as a member of the then JGr.101. Now *Staffelkapitän* of 4./ZG 1, he survived the crash-landing at Trier on 24 May caused by battle damage incurred on a *freie Jagd* sweep, and would be back to lead his *Staffel* in the Battle of Britain.

Another crash 48 hours later had more tragic consequences. By this time, over a fortnight into the campaign, most, if not all, of the *Zerstörergruppen* had moved forward into occupied territory to keep pace with the advancing ground forces, I./ZG 2 having taken up temporary residence at Neufchateau, in Belgium. Here, on 26 May, the *Gruppe* suffered a nuisance raid by a pair of RAF Blenheims. This affront was too much for *Kommandeur* Major Johannes Gentzen. Urgently motioning the *Gruppenadjutant* to follow him, he raced for the *Stabschwarm*'s one serviceable

ZG 26 was another unit involved in the headlong pursuit across France. Taxying out of its camouflaged revetment for yet another sortie, '3U+LN' sports two badges on its nose – the white 'Clog' of II. *Gruppe* and the 'Ace-of-Spades' of 5. *Staffel*

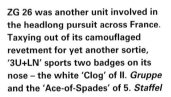

Epitomising the spirit of *'freie Jagd'*, this unidentified machine of ZG 26 hunts among the scattered clouds. The crews of aircraft such as this little realised at the time that the height of the Battle of France also marked the apogee of the Bf 110's career as a daylight *Zerstörer*

Five victory bars adorn the tailfin of another as-yet unidentified ZG 26 aircraft 'somewhere in France'. Also bearing the individual letter 'A', both this machine and the one above were probably flown by *Staffelkapitäne*

Bf 110. Both men climbed aboard and roared off in pursuit of the departing Blenheims.

In their haste, neither man had strapped themselves in properly. The tail of the straining Bf 110 clipped the tops of the trees bordering the airfield and the machine cartwheeled into the ground, killing the two occupants instantly. The Luftwaffe's very first ace was no more.

'Sharksmouths' of II./ZG 76 overfly the smoking ruins of Dunkirk. The BEF has been forced into evacuation, and the first half of the Battle of France has been won

A war photographer captured the activity at a forward base occupied by I./ZG 52 as the unit prepares to take off on another mission. 1. *Staffel*'s 'A2+BH' appears to be the lead aircraft . . .

. . . perhaps because of the *Staffelkapitän*'s 'temporary indisposition'? At first glance, '*Anton-Heinrich*' would seem to have fallen victim to a retaliatory Allied bombing attack, but a close inspection of the original print reveals tell-tale twisted propeller blades. It was presumably either a botched take-off, or heavy landing, which wrenched the tail completely off 'A2+AH' and left it in this rather undignified position

The threat of enemy air raids was, however, obviously taken seriously. Here, another of the *Gruppe*'s machines is being carefully camouflaged among a small stand of saplings

In this last week of May, with the evacuation of Dunkirk getting into its stride, aerial activity was centered firmly along the Channel Coast. In stark contrast to the soldiers of the BEF, who complained bitterly about the absence of the RAF over Dunkirk, *Zerstörer* pilots returning from the coast spoke of the skies being 'full of enemy aircraft'. I./ZG 1 and I./ZG 52 both suffered multiple losses in the area, whilst other pilots who

survived their first brush with RAF Spitfires began to realise just how unmanoeuvrable and vulnerable their Bf 110s really were.

Yet, surprisingly, the casualties were not all one-sided. On 31 May a single *Schwarm* from 5./ZG 26, led by their *Staffelkapitän* (and future *Zerstörer* ace) Oberleutnant Theodor Rossiwall, reportedly bounced an untidy gaggle of Spitfires ten times their number off Dunkirk and shot five of them into the Channel! The next day II./ZG 76 went two better, claiming seven RAF fighters destroyed, including one directly above the evacuation beaches. Following his victim down, Oberleutnant Heinz Nacke had the satisfaction of seeing the Spitfire crash in flames among the dunes, but then had to run the gauntlet of small-arms fire from the incensed soldiery below.

The evacuation of the BEF from France, completed by midnight 2/3 June, signalled the end of the first part of the campaign in the west. It had cost the *Zerstörerwaffe* over 60 Bf 110s. The remaining three weeks until the final cease-fire, which were occupied mainly in harrying a steadily retreating French Army, resulted in far fewer casualties. Some half-dozen *Zerstörer* were lost in combat with fighters of the *Armée de l'Air*... while another five were shot down by the Swiss Air Force!

Srrictly neutral, the Swiss had

Declared an open city, Paris made an ideal backdrop for this propaganda shot showing a *Schwarm* of V.(Z)/LG 1 machines over the Arc de Triomphe (bottom left). A wartime censor has tried to 'doctor' this photograph, but has succeeded merely in partially obliterating the individual aircraft letters. The *Gruppe* badge and otherwise full unit codes are still clearly visible

Harrying the French army southwards, the pilot of this Bf 110 banks low over what appears to be a Somua S-35 tank caught in the open on a country road

A *Rotte* of ZG 26 aircraft illustrates the efficacy of the *Zerstörer*'s new, lighter camouflage scheme. The dark-green machine in the background stands out quite sharply (admittedly it happens to be silhouetted against a fortuitous wisp of cloud!), whereas the dappled finish of 5. *Staffel*'s '3U+HN' at lower right blends in remarkably well with the typically continental agricultural landscape below

jealously guarded their neutrality from the very start, and the French campaign had seen a marked increase in the number of foreign aircraft overflying her territory. Particular culprits were He 111 bombers of the Luftwaffe. Often damaged during raids on southern France, and anxious to reach their home bases, they did not hesitate to shave a few kilometres off the return flight by crossing the Swiss salient west of Basle. The Swiss were equally quick to defend their airspace, attacking such intruders whenever possible, and bringing several down.

An irate Hermann Göring decided to teach them a lesson, and II./ZG 1 was despatched southwards to do the job. On 4 June 28 Bf 110s escorted a single He 111 across the Jura mountains in a deliberate attempt to entice Swiss fighters over France. When this failed, the German formation itself ventured across the neutral border. It was immediately engaged by the watchful Bf 109Es of the Swiss Air Force. The resultant combats ended with honours even – one Bf 109E and one Bf 110 being shot down.

Four days later Hauptmann Dickoré's *Gruppe* was ordered to try again. After somewhat unsportingly bringing down a lone Swiss EKW C-35 reconnaissance machine over Pruntrut, the three *Staffeln* of II./ZG 1 formed into three separate defensive circles, stacked 2000, 4000 and 6000 metres above the Swiss Jura, and awaited developments. They were not long in coming. A patrol of Swiss Bf 109Es arrived overhead, diving down on the defensive circles from an altitude of 7000 metres. Again a Swiss fighter was lost, the badly wounded pilot managing to crash-land his *Emil* at Bözingen-Biel, but this time four Bf 110s failed to return. Wisely perhaps, Generalfeldmarschall Göring did not insist on a third attempt.

FIRST REVERSAL

Bf 110 ZERSTÖRER UNITS IN THE BATTLE OF BRITAIN
– 13 AUGUST 1940

Luftflottenkommando 2 HQ: Brussels

		Base	Est-Serv
Jagdfliegerführer 2 (Wissant)			
Stab ZG 26	Obstlt Joachim-Friedrich Huth	Lille	3-3
I./ZG 26	Hpt Wilhelm Makrocki	Yvrench-St Omer	39-33
II./ZG 26	Hpt Ralph von Rettberg	Crécy-St Omer	37-32
III./ZG 26	Hpt Johann Schalk	Barly-Arques	35-24
Stab ZG 76	Maj Walter Grabmann	Laval	2-0
II./ZG 76	Maj Erich Groth	Abbeville-Yvrench	24-6
III./ZG 76	Hpt Friedrich-Karl Dickoré	Laval	12-11

Luftflottenkommando 3 HQ: Paris

		Base	Est-Serv
VIII. Fliegerkorps (Deauville)			
V.(Z)/LG 1	Hpt Horst Liensberger	Caen	43-29
Jagdfliegerführer 3 (Deauville)			
Stab ZG 2	Obstlt Friedrich Vollbracht	Toussus-le-Noble	4-3
I./ZG 2	Hpt Eberhard Heinlein	Caen-Carpiquet	41-35
II./ZG 2	Maj Harry Carl	Guyancourt	41-34

Luftflottenkommando 5 HQ: Stavanger

		Base	Est-Serv
X. Fliegerkorps (Stavanger)			
I./ZG 76	Hpt Werner Restemeyer	Stavanger-Forus	34-32
		Total	315-242

If the *Zerstörers'* recent advance to the Channel coast had shown up the first chinks in the Bf 110's armour, then coming operations across this narrow stretch of water and beyond into the skies of southern England were to blow the reputation of Göring's vaunted 'Ironsides' wide open.

A first subtle shift of emphasis had already occurred at the close of the French campaign. An increase in the number of RAF bombing raids on Germany by night had obviously prompted someone in the RLM to take a closer look at the report penned by one Hauptmann Wolfgang Falck, describing the rudimentary nightfighting experiments which had been carried out by his *Zerstörergruppe* during their brief sojourn in Denmark in April.

The outcome was perhaps not quite what Falck had expected, for after rampaging through Belgium and France, via Asch, Nivelles, Vendeville and Abbeville, I./ZG 1 had arrived on the coast at Le Havre. Here, Falck was suddenly ordered to about-face and return to Germany with two of his *Staffeln* to set up the Luftwaffe's first official nightfighter *Gruppe* (1./ZG 1 remained in France to provide the nucleus for new experimental fighter-bomber wing, *Erprobungs-gruppe* 210.)

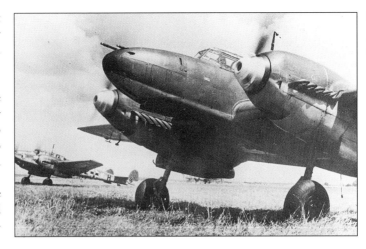

The original German caption to this photograph describes it as portraying 'Bf 110s of I./ZG 52 about to take off on a sortie against England'. By the start of the Battle of Britain, however, the *Gruppe* had been redesignated II./ZG 2, although – as witness 'A2+KH' in the background – the original unit badge and fuselage codes were still being worn

I./ZG 1's abrupt disappearance from the scene left II./ZG 1 somewhat in limbo. The opportunity was therefore taken to redesignate Hauptmann Dickoré's unit to provide a III. *Gruppe* for ZG 76. The only other change of identity at this juncture was I./ZG 52's redesignation as II./ZG 2. It was thus a more tidily organised *Zerstörerwaffe* which was now arrayed against England. What none could yet know was that it was also the last time that the *Zerstörer* force would take to the field as a cohesive whole. The depredations of the weeks ahead would finally prove once and for all that the concept of the heavy fighter, as embodied in the Bf 110, was unsustainable.

Although individual successes would be achieved, and some personal scores would continue to mount, the story of the *Zerstörer* in the Battle of Britain consists of little more than a steady catalogue of losses. At its end, many more *Gruppen* would follow I./ZG 1 into the nightfighter arm (where the Bf 110 was to find its true niche), while others would be redeployed in the fighter-bomber role. The total failure of the Me 210 as the Bf 110's intended replacement, however, meant that the latter would have to be used to equip the resurrected *Zerstörergeschwader* of the mid-war years, and would continue in first-line service until mid-1944.

The first phase of the Battle was aimed at denying the English Channel to British shipping. To this end, a special mixed force battle-group of Do 17 bombers and Ju 87 Stukas was set up, complete with its own Bf 109 escort. Although no *Zerstörergruppe* was actually attached to this command, Bf 110 operations were often flown in conjunction with, and in support of, its activities. The *Zerstörer* thus spent the last three weeks of July 1940 over the Channel and England's south coast harbour towns. Even at this early stage, the three constants which would mark the Bf 110's passage through the Battle were already in evidence – the defensive circle, mounting losses and exaggerated claims of enemy aircraft destroyed.

First, the defensive circle. RAF pilots spoke of *Zerstörer*'s 'forming circles at the drop of a hat'. On 10 July some 30 Bf 110s of III./ZG 26 did just that at the approach of three Hurricanes! In fairness, however, it should be pointed out that the so-called 'defensive circle' was also a decoy manoeuvre, filling a large area of the sky with a prominent mass of wheeling aircraft. Such 'beehives' tended to attract enemy fighters like magnets,

All three *Gruppen* of ZG 26 were heavily involved over southern England. Here, Hauptmann Ralph von Rettberg, *Gruppenkommandeur* of II./ZG 26, briefs his assembled crews for the next mission. The unit's 'Clog' emblem is prominently displayed on the pennant, which was always 'flown' outside *Gruppe* HQ

and thus often served their major purpose, which was to relieve pressure on the accompanied bombers.

Incidentally, RAF Spitfires and Hurricanes attacking these formations would then sometimes be bounced by higher-flying Bf 109s, which helped give rise to the widely-held belief that the long-range fighters had themselves to be provided with a fighter escort. The defensive circle was also occasionally employed as a means of progress combined with the greatest safety, the whole swirling throng slowly 'advancing' towards its given objective.

But despite these measures the *Zerstörergruppen* immediately began to suffer increasing combat losses, small in number at first, but nonetheless disturbing – one aircraft each lost by III./ZG 26 and V.(Z)/LG 1 on 9 July, three by III./ZG 26 on 10 July and four by

III./ZG 26's badge was a ladybird on a diamond, which is seen here adorning one of the unit's Bf 110s. Note, also, the thin coat of washable white paint applied to the aircraft's nose. This latter – a temporary tactical marking – was carried by a number of ZG 26 *Zerstörer* during the Battle of Britain

Not content, it seems, just with their famous 'Sharksmouth', some crews of II./ZG 76 took to painting the flags of the nations they had fought against (or had been based in) below the cockpit of their aircraft. This 5. *Staffel* machine ('M8+BN') already bears the flags of Belgium and France. As the *Gruppe*'s campaigning lengthened, so too did the row of flags. Upon their return to the North Sea after service in the Mediterranean, some aircraft displayed as many as nine – Belgium, France, Great Britain, Holland, Greece, Iraq, Yugoslavia, Norway and Denmark!

III./ZG 76 on 11 July. Among the latter was the Bf 110 flown by Oberleutnant Hans-Joachim Göring, nephew of the Generalfeldmarschall, which cratered into the heights overlooking the naval dockyard in Portland Harbour after a fatal skirmish with No 87 Sqn Hurricanes over Weymouth Bay.

Regarding the overinflated claims of enemy aircraft destroyed, this was by no means restricted to the *Zerstörerwaffe*, nor even to the Luftwaffe as a whole. In the heat of battle, and no doubt in all good faith, both sides overestimated the number of kills actually scored. The problem was perhaps exacerbated by the *Zerstörers'* tendency to fight in formation – at least at the start of an engagement – when several or more claims could be made all for the same victim. Even so, III./ZG 26's claiming of 12 enemy fighters downed in the action of 10 July does seem to border on the overly optimistic, for the only RAF loss of the day was a Hurricane, which collided with a Dornier!

Notwithstanding (or perhaps because of?) the above, new names soon began to emerge as pilots claimed their fifth victories, while older hands continued to add to their scores. 8./ZG 26 seemed particularly successful during this period, *Staffelkapitän* Oberleutnant 'Conny' Meyer being one of those to reach five before the end of July, whilst Sophus Baagoe took his tally to seven.

Having accomplished the virtual closure of the Channel, the Luftwaffe began to prepare for *Adlertag* (Eagle Day), which would set in motion the next phase of the offensive against Great Britain, and was intended to wrest aerial supremacy from the RAF.

In the days leading up to *Adlertag*, the *Zerstörergruppen* were engaged in some heavy fighting. On 8 August, during one of the last major convoy battles, I./ZG 2 and V.(Z)/LG 1 had been credited with 18 kills. Seventy-two hours later, I. and II./ZG 2 formed part of the escort for the largest cross-Channel bombing raid yet mounted by the Luftwaffe. Despite

A *Schwarm* of II./ZG 76 Bf 110s sets off from their Channel Island base for another mission over southern England

Many *Zerstörer* were brought down over England, whilst others were so badly damaged that they did not make it back across the Channel. Few had their demise captured so graphically on film as 'Yellow(?) G', pictured here. References differ as to the aircraft's exact identity, one source stating that this dramatic telephoto sequence, shot from the French side of the Channel, shows the final moments of a 6./ZG 76 machine piloted by Feldwebel Jakob Birndorfer. If this is the case, the incident must have occurred early in the Battle and the crew rescued, for Birndorfer was subsequently killed on crash-landing on the Isle of Wight on 15 August 1940 (in aircraft 'M8+BP', the topmost one of the *Kette* pictured on page 34). Another source suggests the Bf 110 may have been Wk-Nr 3263 of III./ZG 26, shot down into the Channel on 25 September. Again, the crew (pictured in the water in the final photo) were rescued unhurt by the *Seenotdienst*

adopting a communal defensive circle some 60 Bf 110s strong, the *Gruppen* lost six of their number, including the formation leader, and *Kommandeur* of I./ZG 2, Major Ernst Ott.

Further to the east on that same 11 August, fighter-bombers of EGr 210 were being escorted by elements of I./ZG 26. Their leader, Hauptmann Johann 'Hans' Kogler, *Staffelkapitän* of 1./ZG 26, was also shot down, although he was duly picked up out of the sea off the Essex coast by the German air-sea rescue service, and would survive to become *Geschwaderkommodore* of ZG 26 four years hence. On the other side of the coin, 12 August saw the fifth victory for Leutnant Rolf Hermichen of 9./ZG 76, a later Knight's Cross recipient and single-seat *Experte*, who would end the war with a total of 64 kills, of which no fewer than 26 were much-prized US heavy bombers.

Adlertag was finally launched on 13 August, but the adverse weather, which had already caused postponements, played havoc with the carefully timed assault. As with the invasion of Norway, recall orders were sent out, which only added to the confusion. ZG 26 dutifully acknowledged and turned back to base, leaving their charges – 74 Do 17s of KG 2 – to battle on alone. Elsewhere, it was the bombers who had received the message. V.(Z)/LG 1 flew to Portland in splendid isolation, not realising that the follow-up waves of Ju 88s of KG 54 were still sitting on their airfields west of Paris!

Although the various *Zerstörergruppen* involved had optimistically claimed the destruction of more than 30 RAF fighters, the reality of *Adlertag* was that it had cost the Luftwaffe 13 Bf 110s. Göring was furious, but still unwilling to accept the obvious failings of his beloved 'Ironsides' as long-range escort fighters (their lack of speed and manoeuvrability were now being cruelly exposed), he chose instead to castigate his unit commanders.

Forty-eight hours later the events of 15 August would do little to improve the mood of the recently elevated Reichsmarschall. This date

After their disastrous foray across the North Sea on 15 August, I./ZG 76 immediately began to replace their unwieldy *'Dackelbauch'* tanks with the smaller, jettisonable type as carried by Unteroffizier Heinz Fresia's 2. *Staffel* machine. Note the *Staffel* badge - another ladybird (see profile 18)

marked perhaps the worst day in the whole history of the *Zerstörer*. At its close almost 30 Bf 110s – the equivalent of an entire *Gruppe* – would have been lost or damaged beyond repair. Among the missing were three *Gruppenkommandeure*.

A highlight of the day's concerted attacks was to have been the surprise blow provided by *Luftflotte 5*'s entry into the battle. It proved to be anything but that. Misled by German Intelligence into believing that the whole of RAF Fighter Command was fully committed in the south, Generaloberst Hans-Jürgen Stumpff launched his Scandinavian-based *Kampfgruppen* across the North Sea to attack a purportedly undefended north-eastern England. They were escorted by 21 Bf 110Ds of Hauptmann Restemeyer's I./ZG 76 from Stavanger.

Made even more cumbersome than the standard *Zerstörer* by their enormous belly tanks, the *'Dackelbäuche'* stood little chance when suddenly confronted off the Northumberland coast by squadrons of Spitfires and Hurricanes. Seven of their number were destroyed, including the aircraft flown by the *Kommandeur*, which was ripped apart by an explosion of gases in the almost exhausted ventral tank after being struck by fire from the Spitfire I flown by future Australian ace, Flg Off Des Sheen, of No 72 Sqn – see *Osprey Aircraft of the Aces 12 - Spitfire Mk I/II Aces 1939-41* for further details.

This aerial shot of 3. *Staffel*'s *'Gustav-Ludwig'* well illustrates the high-visibility properties of the temporary white markings applied to many ZG 26 aircraft

Although devoid of any tactical markings, 'U8+AH' of 1./ZG 26 displays evidence of a previous fuselage code on its *hellblau* flanks. It is not known, however, whether *'Anton-Heinrich'* is a new machine with its factory-applied four-letter coding now overpainted, or whether it is a replacement aircraft from another unit

One of the fifteen Bf 110s lost by ZG 26 on 18 August 1940 –the 'Hardest Day' – was Leutnant Hans-Joachim Kästner's '3U+EP', which crash-landed near Newchurch, in Kent, after being damaged by RAF fighters

Another who failed to return that day was Oberleutnant Rüdiger Proske, *Gruppenadjutant* of I./ZG 26. Proske inherited 'U8+BB' from the previous incumbent, Günther Specht, who had been wounded in France. Forced down near Lydd, also in Kent, the machine's four MG 17 machine guns have already been removed. But despite the missing upper cowling, part of the *Gruppenstab*'s emblem is clearly visible, as too is the 'winged pencil', Specht's wry pictorial comment on his desk duties (see profile 10)

It was little recompense that surviving members of the *Gruppe* (among them future nightfighter aces Reinhold Eckhardt, Gustav Uellenbeck and Helmut Woltersdorf, and *Jagdwaffe Experten* Gordon Gollob and Leo Schuhmacher) claimed at least nine enemy fighters downed – especially had it been known at the time that the RAF's only total loss was a single crash-landed Hurricane! Not surprisingly, no further such raids across the North Sea were attempted. And by early September I./ZG 76 had left Norway for the Homeland, thus becoming the second *Zerstörergruppe* to be redeployed as a nightfighter unit.

On 16 August 'only' eight Bf 110s were lost. One of them was the aircraft piloted by Major Harry Carl of II./ZG 2, which crashed on landing back in France after suffering damage over the Channel. Neither occupant survived, Carl thus becoming the second ZG 2 *Gruppenkommandeur* to be killed in the space of five days. 16 August was also the date on which Flt Lt J B Nicolson of No 249 Sqn won the only VC ever to be awarded to a pilot of Fighter Command when he remained in his blazing Hurricane to down a Bf 110 near Gosport. Unfortunately, postwar records offer little clue as to the identity of the *Zerstörer* unit involved in the action.

A lull on 17 August served to accentuate the casualties suffered 24 hours later when ZG 26 lost 15 Bf 110s on what has since been called the

Battle's 'Hardest Day'. Initially listed among the missing was Hauptmann Herbert Kaminski, *Staffelkapitän* of 2./ZG 26. However, he and his rear gunner had, in fact, both survived their ditching in the Channel off Dunkirk and were subsequently picked up by a German naval minesweeper. Awarded the Knight's Cross in the interim, Kaminski – nicknamed 'The Last of the Prussians' – would later head II./ZG 76 during the desperate days of 1943-44 in the 'doomed' defence of the Reich.

Throughout this sorry catalogue

49

The 'Sharksmouths'' four leading *Experten,* and all future Knight's Cross holders. They are, from left to right, Oberleutnants Hans-Joachim Jabs and Wilhelm Herget (both of 6./ZG 76), Hauptmann Erich Groth *(Gruppenkommandeur* II./ZG 76) and Hauptmann Heinz Nacke *(Staffelkapitän* 6./ZG 76)

of losses, individual pilots continued to add to their scores. Leutnant Botho Sommer and Feldwebel Walter Scherer, both of III./ZG 76, each managed to claim their fifth kills on 18 August, whilst the *Gruppe*'s top scorer, Oberleutnant Baagoe, maintained his overall lead by taking his total to nine. The rising star of neighbouring II./ZG 76 was one Hans-Joachim Jabs, a future nightfighter *Experte*, and winner of the Oak Leaves.

After 18 August there was a marked reduction in the number of *Zerstörer* operations. Their seeming absence has often been equated with the simultaneous disappearance from the Battle of the Ju 87 – see *Osprey Combat Aircraft 1 - Ju 87 Stukageschwader 1937-41*. But whereas the Stuka *had* to be withdrawn because it simply could not survive in the hostile environment over southern England in the late summer of 1940, the reason for the decrease in Bf 110 activity was much more mundane. Replacements were not keeping pace with losses. There were just not enough *Zerstörer* available.

Nevertheless, Göring insisted that operations be continued, decreeing that twin-engined fighters were to be employed 'where the range of single-engined machines is not sufficient'. In effect, he was sending his *Zerstörer* even deeper into the lion's den. Exactly how they were to carry out this order, while at the same time avoiding further crippling losses, the Reichsmarschall did not deign to make clear. His one edict that, in order to instil a keener sense of aggression, the well-known defensive circle manoeuvre should instead be termed an 'offensive circle', was received by the crews in something akin to stunned silence!

It was not the lack of aggression, but lack of numbers, which kept *Zerstörer* losses down to a minimum for the next few days. But on 25 August nine Bf 110s were lost, five of them machines of ZG 2 tasked with escorting Ju 88s over Dorset. Five days later the target was the Vauxhall factory at Luton. This time it was II./ZG 76 which suffered the heaviest casualties, including one *Staffelkapitän* killed and another (Heinz Nacke) injured. This was also the operation which cost the life of 4. *Staffel*'s Oberfeldwebel Georg Anthony, whose three victories over the *Armée de l'Air* were recounted earlier.

The last day of August offered a rare moment of collective success for the *Zerstörer*. V.(Z)/LG 1 and III./ZG 26 escorted Do 17 bombing raids on Debden and Duxford respectively, and not only were bomber losses minimal, but the Bf 110s' claims for 13 RAF fighters shot down were not far off the mark either. They themselves lost three aircraft, with another five suffering damage. Among the latter was the machine of III./ZG 26's Technical Officer, which crash-landed back at Arques. But the pilot, Oberleutnant Georg Christl, was uninjured, and he would later lead the *Gruppe* with great success in North Africa.

Despite the Reichsmarschall's exhortations, the scale of *Zerstörer* operations declined inexorably during September as the *Gruppen* continued to suffer attrition. The month was topped and tailed by the heaviest casualties – 15 aircraft being lost on both 4 and 27 September. Yet some individual scores continued to climb. A fourth name to join the triumphirate of Baagoe, Jabs and Nacke on the list of *Zerstörer* pilots whose number of victories reached double figures in 1940 was 6./ZG 76's Oberleutnant Wilhelm Herget, who was also destined to achieve later fame in the nightfighter arm.

However, unlike their brethren in the *Jagdwaffe*, many of whom were already highly-decorated household names, the first *Zerstörer* aces remained relatively little known to the German public at large, and came a poor second in the medal stakes. Many, since Falck, had received the Iron Cross, First Class. But there it had stopped. And now that the time had finally come to award the first *Zerstörer* Knight's Crosses, the Reichsmarschall (presumably on the carrot and stick principle?) chose to bestow them upon his unit commanders – the very officers he had berated only weeks earlier for their 'poor leadership'!

The *Zerstörerwaffe*'s first three Knight's Crosses, awarded in September 1940, thus all went to senior *Geschwaderkommodore* – Joachim-Friedrich Huth, late of ZG 26 and recently appointed to the post of *Jagdfliegerführer 2*, Johann Schalk, who had replaced Huth at the head of ZG 26, and Walter Grabmann of ZG 76 (the latter, it should be pointed out, having by now added six more victories to the six he had scored in Spain).

Four of the six other Knight's Crosses presented before the end of 1940 similarly went to higher commanders, three of them to *Gruppenkommandeure* who were also aces in their own right. Only two were awarded to the relatively lowly. Uniquely, both were members of 6./ZG 76, namely *Staffelkapitän* Hauptmann Heinz Nacke for his 12 victories, and acting *Staffelführer* Oberleutnant Hans-Joachim Jabs, who had taken over after Nacke was injured, and whose 19 kills made him the *Zerstörer*'s current top scorer.

In all truth, it was little enough official recognition for a force which had a year's hard campaigning behind it – a force which had surpassed all expectations in Poland, excelled itself over the German Bight and Norway, fulfilled its role in France, and been fought almost to extinction over England.

Numbers never tell the whole story, but one Battle of Britain statistic is as stark as it is sobering. The Luftwaffe had embarked upon the Battle with 237 serviceable Bf 110 *Zerstörer* . . . and lost no fewer than 223 in the waging of it.

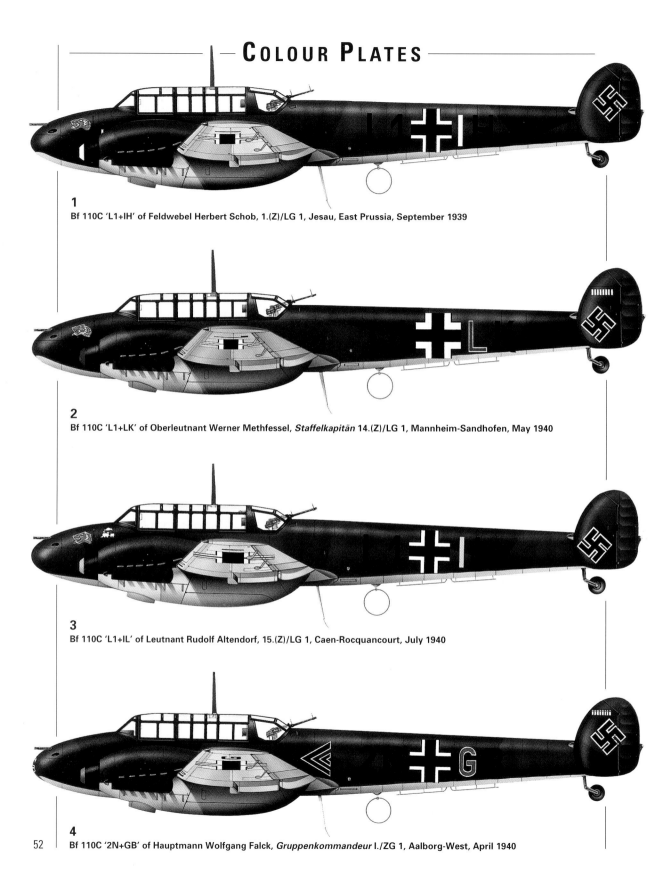

1
Bf 110C 'L1+IH' of Feldwebel Herbert Schob, 1.(Z)/LG 1, Jesau, East Prussia, September 1939

2
Bf 110C 'L1+LK' of Oberleutnant Werner Methfessel, *Staffelkapitän* 14.(Z)/LG 1, Mannheim-Sandhofen, May 1940

3
Bf 110C 'L1+IL' of Leutnant Rudolf Altendorf, 15.(Z)/LG 1, Caen-Rocquancourt, July 1940

4
Bf 110C '2N+GB' of Hauptmann Wolfgang Falck, *Gruppenkommandeur* I./ZG 1, Aalborg-West, April 1940

5
Bf 110C '2N+BB' of Oberleutnant Siegfried Wandam, *Gruppenadjutant* I./ZG 1, Vendeville, May 1940

6
Bf 110G 'S9+IC' of Hauptmann Günther Tonne, *Gruppenkommandeur* II./ZG 1, Byelgorod-II, Ukraine, June 1942

7
Bf 110C '3M+AA' of Oberstleutnant Friedrich Vollbracht, *Geschwaderkommodore* ZG 2, Toussus-le-Noble, August 1940

8
Bf 110C '3U+AA' of Oberstleutnant Johann Schalk, *Geschwaderkommodore* ZG 26, Memmingen, January 1941

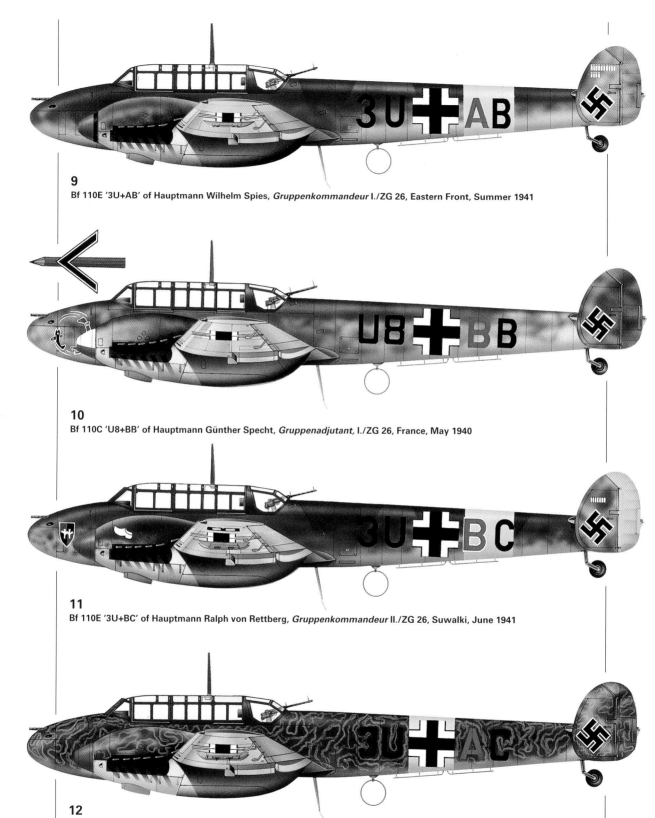

9
Bf 110E '3U+AB' of Hauptmann Wilhelm Spies, *Gruppenkommandeur* I./ZG 26, Eastern Front, Summer 1941

10
Bf 110C 'U8+BB' of Hauptmann Günther Specht, *Gruppenadjutant,* I./ZG 26, France, May 1940

11
Bf 110E '3U+BC' of Hauptmann Ralph von Rettberg, *Gruppenkommandeur* II./ZG 26, Suwalki, June 1941

12
Bf 110E '3U+AC' of Hauptmann Werner Thierfelder, *Gruppenkommandeur* II./ZG 26, Smolensk Sector, January 1942

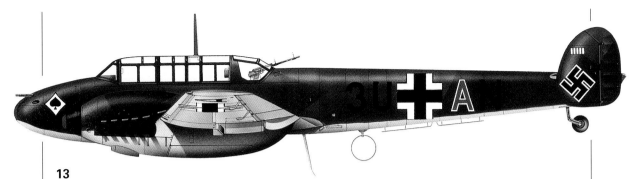

13
Bf 110C '3U+AN' of Oberleutnant Theodor Rossiwall, *Staffelkapitän* 5./ZG 26, St Trond, May 1940

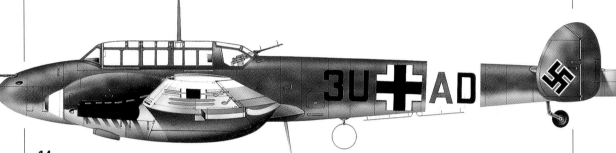

14
Bf 110D '3U+AD' of Hauptmann Georg Christl, *Gruppenkommandeur* III./ZG 26, North Africa, January 1942

15
Bf 110E '3U+AR' of Oberleutnant Georg Christl, *Staffelkapitän* of 7./ZG 26, Taranto, Italy, April 1941

16
Bf 110E '3U+FR' of Oberleutnant Alfred Wehmeyer, *Staffelkapitän* of 7./ZG 26, Derna, May 1942

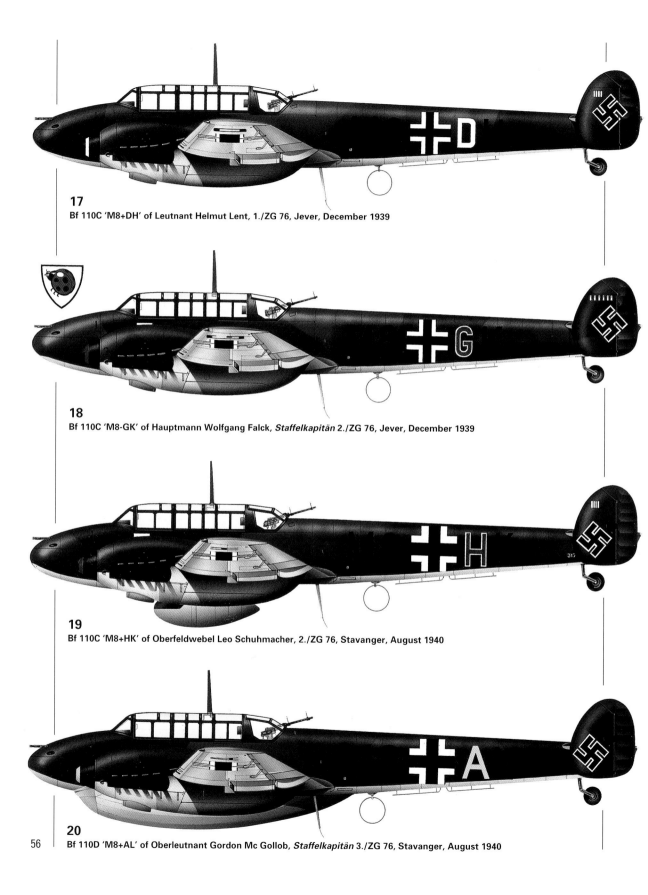

17

Bf 110C 'M8+DH' of Leutnant Helmut Lent, 1./ZG 76, Jever, December 1939

18

Bf 110C 'M8-GK' of Hauptmann Wolfgang Falck, *Staffelkapitän* 2./ZG 76, Jever, December 1939

19

Bf 110C 'M8+HK' of Oberfeldwebel Leo Schuhmacher, 2./ZG 76, Stavanger, August 1940

20

Bf 110D 'M8+AL' of Oberleutnant Gordon Mc Gollob, *Staffelkapitän* 3./ZG 76, Stavanger, August 1940

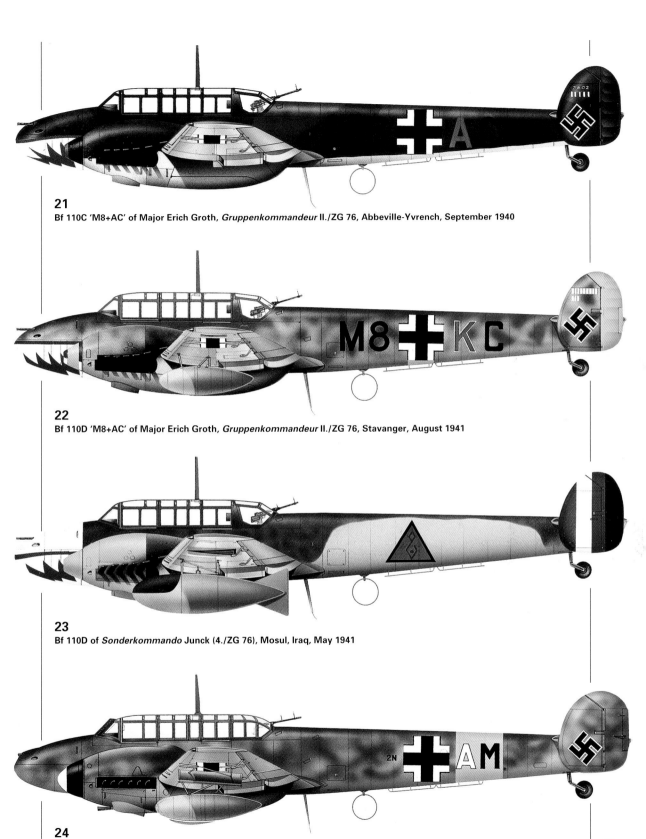

21
Bf 110C 'M8+AC' of Major Erich Groth, *Gruppenkommandeur* II./ZG 76, Abbeville-Yvrench, September 1940

22
Bf 110D 'M8+AC' of Major Erich Groth, *Gruppenkommandeur* II./ZG 76, Stavanger, August 1941

23
Bf 110D of *Sonderkommando* Junck (4./ZG 76), Mosul, Iraq, May 1941

24
Bf 110G '2N+AM' of Oberleutnant Helmut Haugk, *Staffelkapitän* 4./ZG 76, Ansbach, March 1944

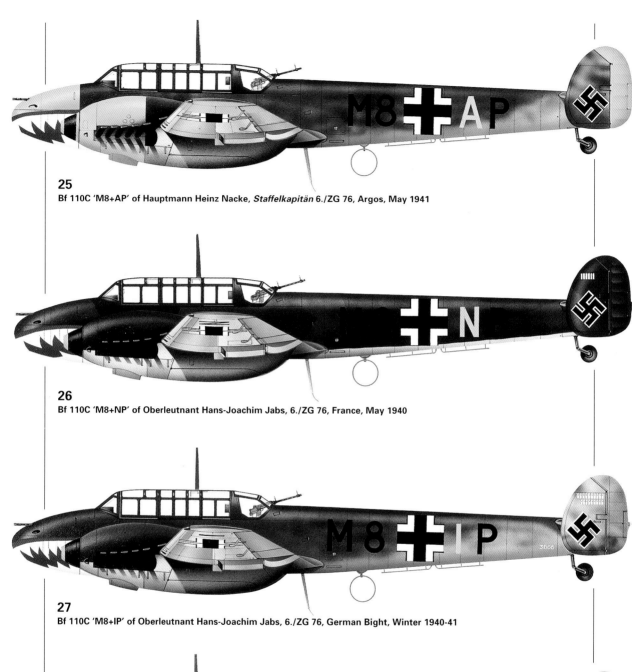

25
Bf 110C 'M8+AP' of Hauptmann Heinz Nacke, *Staffelkapitän* 6./ZG 76, Argos, May 1941

26
Bf 110C 'M8+NP' of Oberleutnant Hans-Joachim Jabs, 6./ZG 76, France, May 1940

27
Bf 110C 'M8+IP' of Oberleutnant Hans-Joachim Jabs, 6./ZG 76, German Bight, Winter 1940-41

28
Bf 110D '2N+DP' of Feldwebel Hans Peterburs, 6./ZG 76, Stavanger, Winter 1940-41

29
Bf 110E 'LN+FR' of Oberleutnant Felix Maria Brandis, *Staffelkapitän* 1.(Z)/JG 77, Rovaniemi, Finland, September 1941

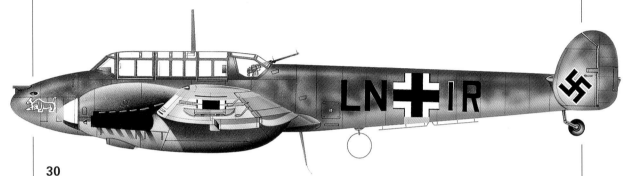

30
Bf 110C 'LN+IR' of Feldwebel Theodor Weissenberger, 1.(Z)/JG 77, Kirkenes, Norway, September 1941

31
Bf 110E 'S9+AH' of Oberleutnant Wolfgang Schenk, *Staffelkapitän* 1./SKG 210, Sechinskaya, September 1941

1
Oberleutnant Werner Methfessel
of 14.(Z)./LG 1, Würzburg, Winter
1939-40

2
Hauptmann Heinz Nacke, *Staffelka-*
pitän of 6./ZG 76, at Jever, Winter
1940-41

3
Oberfeldwebel Richard Heller of
III./ZG 26, Mediterranean theatre,
September 1941

4
Hauptmann Theodor Rossiwall,
Staffelkapitän of 5./ZG 26 on the
Eastern Front, Autumn 1941

5
Oberleutnant Felix Maria Brandis,
Staffelkapitän of 1.(Z)./JG 77, at
Rovaniemi, Winter 1941-42

6
Major Eduard Tratt, *Gruppenkom-
mandeur* of II./ZG 26 at Hildesheim,
Autumn 1943

THE STEADY DECLINE

Bf 110 UNITS IN THE BALKANS CAMPAIGN, 5 APRIL 1941

Luftflottenkommando 4 HQ: Vienna

		Base	Type	Est-Serv
Fliegerführer Arad (Arad/Rumania)				
I./ZG 26	Hpt Wilhelm Makrocki	Szeged	Bf 110C/E	33-30
VIII. Fliegerkorps (Gorna Djunmaya/Bulgaria)				
II./ZG 26	Hpt Ralph von Rettberg	Krainici	Bf 110C/E	37-25

The end of the Battle of Britain was to lead to the dismemberment of the *Zerstörerwaffe*. Incapable of holding its own against determined single-engined fighter attack, except under only the most advantageous of circumstances, the Bf 110 needed to be found new employment. Three *Gruppen* were therefore returned to an earlier, and more suitable, role – coastal patrol and convoy escort, where the only opposition likely to be encountered would be small formations of enemy bombers. III./ZG 76 had already left the Channel coast in October, transferring to Stavanger, in Norway, to replace the departed I./ZG 76. II./ZG 76 and III./ZG 26 were also earmarked for similar overwater patrol and escort duties in the German Bight and the Mediterranean respectively.

The Battle had also finally brought to an end Göring's long infatuation with the *Zerstörer*. The Reichsmarschall was not only bitterly disappointed at his 'Ironsides'' poor showing, he now had other priorities. The growing strength of RAF night raids on Germany reflected badly on the Luftwaffe's inability to counter them, and to bolster the Reich's nocturnal defences, all five of the remaining *Zerstörergruppen* would be incorporated into the nightfighter arm over the coming months.

Thus by early 1941, when Hitler's mind was firmly focused on the forthcoming offensive against the Soviet Union, the once tight-knit *Zerstörerwaffe* had been backwatered into a purely defensive collection of disparate and widely dispersed units. But then events in the Balkans took a hand. Mussolini's untimely attack on Albania, and the uncertain allegiance of Yugoslavia, forced the *Führer* to intervene. *Luftflotte 4* was ordered to assemble an aerial strike force to support the ground troops' invasions of Yugoslavia and Greece. Suddenly, there was a need again for a long-range fighter. I. and II./ZG 26, which had already been redesignated as I. and II./NJG 4, quickly reverted to their original identities before being sent to south-east Europe. A II. *Gruppe* chronicler noted:

'The transfer to Bulgaria was an absolute joy. The *Staffeln* flew in stages via Vienna, Debrecen and some unpronounceable place in Rumania. At each stop there was a few days' wait for the groundcrews to catch up by rail. Three days and nights were spent in Debrecen as the guests of the Hungarian Air Force. The tables groaned with every type of local delicacy you could think of: salami sausage, Tokay wine, stuffed duck, roast goose, fruit schnapps. And when the time came to take off on the next leg, there was a large packet of sausages in every cockpit - long live *Ungarland*!'

But the groundcrews had to fend for themselves. One party had been sitting in their unheated carriages on the Hungarian-Rumanian frontier for five days, awaiting the arrival of a Rumanian locomotive, when a second column was shunted in alongside them. The new arrivals were sympathetic and generous with the wine they had been purchasing en route. When the members of the first column nursed their hangovers into life next morning, they found themselves on their own again. A locomotive had arrived during the night, but a carton of cigarettes had persuaded its driver to hitch up the wrong train. The original party eventually had to be collected by road, the Rumanian authorities flatly refusing to provide them with another locomotive – and even accusing the unfortunate individual in charge of selling the first one!

On 6 April the Balkans campaign opened in the north with a savage series of bombing raids on Belgrade. Escorting the bombers, I./ZG 26 thus became the second *Zerstörergruppe* to face foreign-flown Bf 109s – this time of the Yugoslav Air Force. Unteroffizier Stiegleder claimed two of the foreign *Emils*, but I./ZG 26 lost five of their own Bf 110s in this day's fighting. Further to the south, II./ZG 26 were supporting 12. *Armee*'s drive out of Bulgaria. Here they encountered Yugoslav Hawker Furies, several of which were shot down. But II. *Gruppe* also suffered casualties, with two Bf 110s failing to return.

Even III./ZG 26 took part in this first day of the campaign. Already based in the Mediterranean, the *Gruppe* was transferred from Sicily to the heel of Italy, from where they flew across the Adriatic Sea to attack targets in central southern Yugoslavia. They too claimed the destruction of a brace of Yugoslav Bf 109s, one of which, brought down south of Sarajevo,

Newly arrived in the Mediterranean, 7./ZG 26 make themselves at home in the welcoming shade of a Sicilian olive grove. Note that the aircraft on the right ('3U+JR') is still wearing what appears to be a Battle of Britain-style white nose

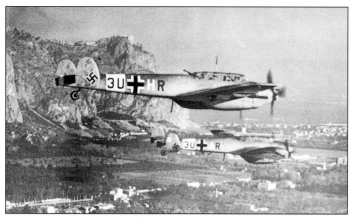

Resplendent in their new Mediterranean theatre livery (a broad white band around the rear fuselage, selected to match *Regia Aeronautica* markings of the period), 'AR' and 'HR' set out to explore their new suroundings

If the original German caption to this photograph is correct, III./ZG 26 also played a part in the invasion of Crete, for this somewhat worse for wear Bf 110 was reportedly brought down by ground fire from the island's defenders. What may appear to be light foliage wrapped around the nose is, in fact, the 'White cockerel' badge of 9. *Staffel* (see photo on page 68)

provided the fifth victory for future desert ace Oberfeldwebel Richard Heller.

In many respects Yugoslavia was a re-run of Poland. After the initial air opposition had been neutralised, the Luftwaffe concentrated on bombing and strafing the enemy's ground forces. For the *Zerstörer* this held true even after the arrival of the RAF and throughout the Wehrmacht's subsequent advance southwards through Greece. Many British aircraft were destroyed or damaged on airfields such as Menidi, Eleusis and Argos by ground-strafing Bf 110s.

But there were also a number of aerial engagements involving the Bf 110. It was one such, on 20 April, which presented the *Zerstörer* with arguably their most prestigious single success. Having escorted a large formation of bombers to Piraeus, II./ZG 26 was released to strafe targets of opportunity in the surrounding areas. RAF Hurricanes from nearby Eleusis rose to give battle, and in the scattered and prolonged action which followed, 5./ZG 26 lost two aircraft but shot down five of the British fighters. Among those credited with kills were *Staffelkapitän* Hauptmann Theodor Rossiwall and Oberleutnant Sophus Baagoe, thereby taking their respective totals to 12 and 14. It is not known, however, exactly whose guns accounted for the Hurricanes, and brought to an end the career of South African Sqn Ldr M T St J 'Pat' Pattle of No 33 Sqn, the highest-scoring RAF pilot of World War 2 with of a tally of at least 50 kills – fellow 6.5-kill ace Flt Lt W J 'Timber' Woods of No 80 Sqn was also lost during this engagement.

By the end of April Athens was in German hands, and preparations were being made for the next phase of the campaign – the invasion of the island of Crete. I. and II./ZG 26 took up residence at Argos, where they were joined by the 'Sharkmouths' of II./ZG 76, transferred down from the German Bight. Once again the *Zerstörer*'s role would be mainly that of low-level attack, strafing the island's ground defences and engaging the ships of the Royal Navy in the surrounding waters. Such operations were both hazardous and costly. More than a dozen Bf 110s would fall victim to a variety of anti-aircraft weapons, ranging from Brens to Bofors, before Crete was finally secured. Two of the losses were felt particularly keenly.

On 14 May the seemingly unstoppable Sophus Baagoe was shot into the sea off the island's northern coast while strafing the

Another *Zerstörer* roars low over Crete's arid terrain, seeking out any remaining pockets of resistance

A line-up of 4./ZG 76 machines at the close of the Balkans campaign. In addition to the bright red 'Sharksmouth', these aircraft also have white upper nose cowlings and yellow engine nacelles! Note, too, the 900-litre underwing fuel tanks. These latter would prove to be essential for the long haul to Iraq, which the *Staffel* was soon to undertake

airfield at Heraklion. His Bf 110 was claimed both by a Gladiator pilot and the field's anti-aircraft defences. Exactly a month later Baagoe would be honoured with a posthumous Knight's Cross. On that same 14 June two other members of the *Geschwader* received the award – Hauptleute Ralph von Rettberg, *Gruppenkommandeur* of II./ZG 26, and Wilhelm Spies, the new leader of I. *Gruppe*.

In the interim the first *Zerstörer* Knight's Cross fatality had occurred. On 21 May a small coastal patrol vessel was being persistently strafed in Suda Bay when one of its ammunition lockers exploded. The attacker, a Bf 110 of I./ZG 26, flew into the debris, clipped the ship's mast and smashed into the water, killing the pilot, *Gruppenkommandeur* Hauptmann Wilhelm Makrocki, and his rear gunner.

Forty eight hours later over the same area, I./ZG 26's Leutnant Johannes Kiel had more success when he claimed several motor torpedo boats sunk or damaged. Twenty-four hours later still, coastal forces redressed the balance somewhat when a Lewis gunner aboard a naval motor launch brought down a Bf 110 of II./ZG 76 south of the island.

After each losing another aircraft apiece prior to the final Allied withdrawal from the island, the three *Zerstörergruppen* involved in the invasion of Crete subsequently returned northwards.

II./ZG 76 resumed their watch on the German Bight, but were destined to be swallowed up by the omnivorous nightfighter arm before the year was out. I. and II./ZG 26 would likewise be reincorporated into the *Nachtjagdwaffe* (whence they had temporarily escaped to participate in the Balkans campaign), but not for another 12 months. First they would provide the sole *Zerstörer* presence in the greatest invasion of all – that of the Soviet Union.

Not all the 'Sharkmouths' of II./ZG 76 returned to the Reich, however. Early in April 1941 a military *coup d'état* in Iraq had brought to power a pro-German government in that country. Anxious to protect her interests in the area, Britain landed some 8000 troops at Basra, in the Persian Gulf, a fortnight later. Iraq retaliated by laying siege to the RAF airfield at Habbaniyah, west of the capital Baghdad, and calling on Hitler for assistance.

Eager to capitalise on the unrest in the Middle East, Foreign Minister Joachim von Ribbentrop urged the immediate despatch of one *Jagd-* and one *Kampfgeschwader*. But with the attack on the Soviet Union now only weeks away, such a large force could ill be spared by the Luftwaffe. Instead, Oberst Werner Junck was summoned to Berlin from his post as *Jagdfliegerführer 3* in occupied France. Arriving in the German capital, Junck was informed that 'the Führer wants to make a heroic gesture'.

Thus was born the *'Sonderkommando* (Special Force) Junck', which comprised one *Staffel* of He 111 bombers (4./KG 4), one *Staffel* of *Zerstörer* (4./ZG 76) and a dozen transports, including a trio of four-engined Ju 90s. In the second week of May 1941, the aircraft of the *'Sonderkommando* began arriving in Iraq. Led by *Staffelkapitän* Oberleutnant Hobein, the 12 Bf 110s of 4./ZG 76 – each carrying a three-man crew, and packed with as much equipment as possible – turned their backs on Crete and staged eastwards, via Rhodes and French Vichy-held Syria, to Mosul, a town in the centre of an important oil field region some 350 km to the north of the Iraqi capital.

The *Zerstörers'* 'campaign' would last all of ten days. During that time, they claimed at least two RAF Gladiators shot down over Habbaniyah, one of which fell to future nightfighter *'Experte'* Leutnant Martin Drewes. But once again the Bf 110s' main occupation was that of ground-strafing, their targets including the RAF base and British troop emplacements and convoys. The *Staffel's* losses were commensurate, and despite cannibalising two machines badly damaged in an RAF counter-raid on Mosul, by 26 May there was not a single serviceable Bf 110 left. The surviving aircrews were evacuated by transport Junkers.

There was an interesting footnote to the Bf 110's short career in Iraq. Neither of the last two serviceable machines, despatched against Habbaniyah on 25 May, had returned to base. One, which had made a successful wheels-up landing not far from the target, was recovered by the

Looking distinctly less than delighted at the prospect, a RAF pilot prepares to take *THE BELLE OF BERLIN* (Wk-Nr 4035) up for a test flight, presumably from Heliopolis in Egypt. The 'Sharksmouth' has obviously been scrubbed off (rumours that it was pinched by No 112 Sqn for use on their Tomahawks at nearby Fayid are a calumny!). This aircraft was captured after belly-landing near Mosul, in Iraq, and following its restoration to airworthiness, was first flown by Sqn Ldr Al Bocking of the Blenheim-equipped No 11 Sqn, which was then based at Habbinyah. The *Zertstörer* was then ferried to Egypt, where it was unofficially adopted by No 267 Sqn at Heliopolis (the latter unit was the base's redesignated Communication Flight) and decorated with its 'KW' codes. The aircraft was subsequently flown for a good number of months until reportedly transferred to No 89 Sqn (flying Beaufighter IFs) in March 1942. It was finally lost in a belly landing at Atbara, in the Sudan, during a ferry flight to South Africa

RAF. Raised back up on its mainwheels by block and tackle, the Bf 110's tail was lashed to a lorry and it was slowly towed back to Habbaniyah – the searing desert sun necessitating frequent stops to pour water on the aircraft's overheating tyres.

Using spare parts salvaged from the wreckage found at Mosul, the Bf 110 was restored to airworthiness and test-flown, both at Habbaniyah and, later, at RAF Heliopolis, near Cairo in Egypt. By now the otherwise anonymous Wk-Nr 4035 had been given the name *THE BELLE OF BERLIN*, and allocated RAF serial HK846. After a thorough examination at Heliopolis, the Bf 110 was to be flown to South Africa to familiarise aircrew under training there with enemy equipment. But the *'BELLE* never made it, for a second belly landing en route, this time in northern Sudan, proved too much for her.

MEDITERRANEAN AND NORTH AFRICA

In direct contrast to 4./ZG 76's ten-day intervention in Iraq, III./ZG 26, as the first *Zerstörergruppe* to be despatched to the Mediterranean, would remain in the same area for over two-and-a-half years, thus making it possibly the longest serving of any Luftwaffe unit in that theatre.

After withdrawing from the Channel coast, III./ZG 26 had first transferred to Neubiberg for re-equipment. From there, they staged

This *Rotte* of III. *Gruppe* Bf 110s is seen guarding an untidy gaggle of supply Ju 52s, some two-dozen strong, as it heads out across the Mediterranean

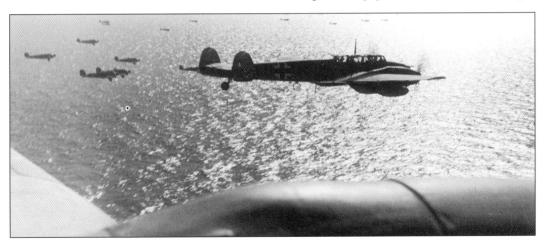

There was little opportunity to pose idyllically in picturesque African oases as this 8. *Staffel* machine is doing, cockpit and mainwheels covered against the blazing heat of the sun

'LT' and 'MT' of 9./ZG 26 go about their daily chores, patrolling Mediterranean airspace. Both machines are sporting 9. *Staffel's* 'Cockerel' badge, with the former is also wearing the 'Ladybird-in-a-diamond' emblem of III. *Gruppe*. The small white 'N' on the nacelle of the nearest aircraft indicates that it is powered by DB 601N engines

southwards late in December 1940, via Treviso in Italy, to the island of Sicily. Commanded by Major Karl Kaschka, the *Gruppe's* tasks in the Mediterranean were manifold. Foremost among them was the safeguarding of the sea and air supply lanes between southern Europe and North Africa. But III./ZG 26 would also be called upon to attack enemy shipping, carry out reconnaissance flights and *freie Jagd* patrols, and support the Axis ground forces during the desert campaign. As mentioned earlier, they also participated in the invasion of Yugoslavia, and would put in several appearances over Malta.

To fulfil all these roles, the *Gruppe's* three component *Staffeln* usually operated independently, and from bases many hundreds of kilometres apart. For example, one *Staffel* would be in Sicily to protect the supply routes from Italy which skirted Malta to the west, whilst another would be in Crete to cover convoys departing Greece and by-passing Malta to the east, while the third would be in North Africa itself. But these dispositions, dictated by the see-saw nature of the desert war, would be continually changing as North African supply ports were won, lost, and won back again, or whenever critical phases of the land fighting demanded additional air support. And whereas in the early months convoy escort duties had been for the most part uneventful (and favourite jaunts of war correspondents and photographers anxious to get 'a real taste of combat flying'), the desert front could almost always be relied upon to provide those elements of the *Gruppe* which happened to be stationed there with some sort of action.

The first encounter between Bf 110s of III./ZG 26 and British fighters took place on 19 February 1941, and resulted in a kill each for two of the *Gruppe's* future Knight's Cross recipients. Escorting Ju 87 Stukas to bomb Tobruk, the *Zerstörers* met Hurricanes of No 3 Sqn, RAAF. Leutnant Alfred Wehmeyer despatched one of the Australians, but was himself shot into the sea (from which he was rescued 24 hours later) by a second Hurricane, which was in turn brought down by Oberfeldwebel Richard Heller.

Tobruk would dominate the activities of III./ZG 26 – more accurately those of 8./ZG 26, the 'resident' Africa *Staffel*, for most of this period – throughout much of the remainder of 1941. It was on 15 July that Richard Heller was flying as a lone pathfinder for a *Gruppe* of Ju 87s sent

Invariably operating in less than ideal conditions, groundcrews' became adept at improvising when in the field. For example, this pair are using an Italian water drum as a makeshift workbench. 9. *Staffel*'s *'Berta-Theodor'* has white and/or yellow nacelles and spinners, and the unit badge superimposed on two vertical chevrons the latter marking was a not uncommon feature found on all three *Staffel* emblems of III./ZG 26, but its exact significance has not been established

to dive-bomb shipping in the Tobruk area when the formation was attacked by a dozen or more Hurricanes. From his position in the lead, Heller pulled round in a wide curve to engage the British fighters from the rear. He shot down three of them in as many minutes and forced the remainder to break away. The Stukas reportedly returned to base without loss. For this action Oberfeldwebel Heller was awarded the Knight's Cross, thus becoming the first of five members of III./ZG 26 to be so honoured during the *Gruppe*'s Mediterranean service.

By mid-November 1941 the Axis offensive which the Bf 110s of III./ZG 26 were supporting (nearly 20 per cent of the *Zerstörers'* desert operations were ground-attack missions) had been brought to a halt. In readiness for the inevitable Allied counter-attack, the entire *Gruppe* was concentrated in North Africa, 7. and 9. *Staffeln* being pulled out of Sicily and Crete respectively to join with 8./ZG 26 at Derna.

Operation *Crusader* (the British bid to recapture Cyrenaica) was launched on 18 November. The Bf 110s suffered heavily in the opening rounds, with a number of aircraft being lost and others badly damaged, including that belly-landed by a wounded Richard Heller after combat with 12 Tomahawks on 24 November. The casualties continued into December, and included two *Gruppenkommandeure*. Major Karl Kaschka was shot down by a Hurricane near Fort Capuzzo on 4 December, whilst his successor, Hauptmann Thomas Steinberger, survived all of 20 days before being lost on a ferry flight (after possibly colliding with a wingman) between Athens and Crete on Christmas Eve. The *Gruppe*'s

A mixed *Schwarm* of 8. and 9. *Staffel* aircraft overflies typical North African coastal terrain

third *Kommandeur* in the space of three weeks was Hauptmann Georg Christl, erstwhile *Gruppo* TO, and of late the *Staffelkapitän* of 7./ZG 26, whose tenure of office was destined to last until the *Zerstörers'* final withdrawal from the Mediterranean.

Two months after the start of *Crusader*, the Allied advance ran out of steam, and the pendulum of the desert war began to swing eastwards

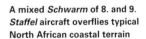

The Bf 110 had other uses. 7./ZG 26's '3U+NR' provides shelter from the noonday sun for a group of Afrika Korps soldiery (newly arrived in the transport Ju's just visible in the background?). The underwing bomb-racks are empty – let's hope that 300-litre fuel tank does not spring a leak!

Perhaps a hardier breed, Allied (Kittyhawk) fighter pilots found an even more novel use for the tailplane of a derelict *Zerstörer*. Never mind the midday sun, just keep the beer coming. By all reports, *'Ye Olde Me 110 Inn'* was a favourite desert watering hole – courtesy, in all likelihood, of III./ZG 26

again as the *Afrika Korps* embarked upon a limited counter-offensive. III./ZG 26's recent losses had resulted in 8. *Staffel*'s withdrawal to Germany for complete re-equipment. And with 9./ZG 26 having returned to Crete, only some half-dozen serviceable machines of 7. *Staffel* remained to support Rommel's latest push. This they did to the best of their limited ability, flying mainly bombing sorties, and suffering in the process.

By early May 1942, 7./ZG 26 was back at Derna. Here, the *Gruppe* was united again (by the arrival of 8. and 9. *Staffeln* from Castel Benito and Crete) and attached, together with the Ju 88 bombers of 12./LG 1, to Major Walter Sigel's *Stukageschwader* 3 to form the *Gefechtsverband* (Combat Command) Sigel.

The role of this self-contained battle-group was to support Rommel's ground troops, whose limited offensive had by now burgeoned into a full-scale advance, as they pushed across Libya and into Egypt. Over the next ten weeks III./ZG 26 staged slowly eastwards in the wake of the land fighting, from Derna to El Alamein. Throughout this period operations remained very much as before, with bomber escort missions and ground-attack sorties being the norm. But one pilot introduced a new element

More activity at 8./ZG 26's 'dispersal', as crated spares and replacement aircraft arrive. The former have already been unpacked (note the pile of handy firewood for those cold desert nights in the left foreground), whilst many of the latter have yet to be adorned with their new unit codes. The Italian CR.42 on the extreme left of the photo appears still to be awaiting a replacement set of wings

when, towards the end of May, Oberleutnant Alfred Wehmeyer, *Staffelkapitän* of 7./ZG 26, tried his hand at nightfighting.

Wehmeyer scored three nocturnal victories – a Wellington on the night of 22-23 May, a Boston near Derna exactly a weeks later, and a second Wellington near the Martuba landing grounds during the night of 31 May/1 June. But this string of successes came to an abrupt end only hours after the latter kill when Wehmeyer's Bf 110 was one of three which failed to return from operations on 1 June, his aircraft having taken a direct hit from an anti-aircraft shell while ground-strafing west of Tobruk. Oberleutnant Wehmeyer would be awarded a posthumous Knight's Cross on 4 September 1942.

In the first week of August, with the opposing armies stalemated at El Alamein, III./ZG 26 was released from the *Gefechtsverband* Sigel. Leaving just one *Staffel* at Derna (supported by the Do 17s of the recently activated 10./ZG 26 at Barce), the bulk of the *Gruppe* transferred back to Crete to resume convoy escort duties, but by now a new adversary had appeared on the Mediterranean anti-shipping scene – heavy bombers of the USAAF.

One of the earliest *Zerstörer* versus four-engined bomber clashes occurred on 21 August 1942 when a pair of Bf 110s of III./ZG 26 intercepted nine Palestinian-based B-24s intent on attacking an Axis convoy to the south-west of Crete. The Bf 110s claimed two bombers destroyed, one of which was seen to crash into the sea. Further such encounters were to follow in the weeks ahead. And the new opposition brought to the fore

'3U+FU' was a relatively intact Do 17Z of 10./ZG 26 abandoned by the retreating Luftwaffe and found by the Allies at Castel Benito. As far as is known, this *Staffel* did not have its own badge. *'Friedrich-Ulrich'* is here seen sporting the *'Horst Wessel'* shield of the parent *Geschwader*

new names from within the *Gruppe*'s ranks. Two NCO pilots in particular, Oberfeldwebel Helmut Haugk and Feldwebel Günther Wegmann, became acknowledged '*Viermot-Experten*', both surviving the war with six heavy bombers apiece included in their final scores.

On 3 September, during the return flight to Crete after a shuttle escort mission to Derna, Wegmann came upon another nine B-24s attacking a supply convoy. On this occasion he was able to claim only one bomber damaged. His own aircraft also suffered hits, but he managed to make it back to Crete and pull off a successful belly-landing. Scrambled on his own four days later in a replacement machine, he chased after a pair of B-24s reported south of the island. He shot one down and damaged the second, but again his own aircraft was hit by return fire. The *Gruppenkommandeur* could perhaps be forgiven if his congratulations on Wegmann's kill and successful return were slightly less than whole-hearted – it was *his* Bf 110 that Wegmann had been flying, and which now had over 50 bullet holes in it!

Towards the end of the month it was Helmut Haugk's turn. Patrolling alone over the eastern Mediterranean on 29 September, he spotted a formation of 11 B-24s and attacked and brought down two of them. Haugk would be the fifth, and final, member of III./ZG 26 to receive the Knight's Cross for service in the Mediterranean theatre on 21 December 1942 – two others, *Gruppenkommandeur* Hauptmann Georg Christl, and Oberleutnant Fritz Schulze-Dickow, *Staffelkapitän* of 8./ZG 26 had been decorated earlier in the year for outstanding leadership during the desert campaigns.

Within days of Haugk's downing the two B-24s, the desert war entered its final phase. Gen Montgomery fought and won the Battle of El Alamein, and the *Afrika Korps* began its long retreat to Tunisia. III./ZG 26 did what they could to assist in the withdrawal and keep the cross-Mediterranean supply lanes open, but in the face of increasing enemy air superiority, it was a time of steady losses – not for adding to scores. After the Allied landings in north-west Africa early in November 1942, the bulk of the *Gruppe* retired to Trapani in Sicily. From here, they continued to escort the

Right up until the very end in Africa, the *Zerstörer* crews' primary role remained that of shepherding and safeguarding the lumbering Ju 52s, whether over land . . .

. . . or over water

fleets of transport Ju 52s carrying reinforcements into Tunisia and evacuating the wounded back to Europe.

Only a few small attachments of Bf 110s remained in Africa. Based at Bizerta, Sousse and Tunis itself, they still claimed the occasional success, most notably against twin-engined P-38s. On 6 February 1943 the *Gruppe* celebrated its 10,000th operational sortie, but in the six months leading up to the final German withdrawal from Tunisia in May 1943, it is estimated that III./ZG 26 had accounted for little more than 20 enemy aircraft destroyed.

The loss of Tunisia resulted in the *Gruppe*'s vacating Sicily for mainland Italy. Stationed around Rome, they were now charged with the protection of central and northern Italy from Allied heavy bomber raids. They had already experienced such raids while at Trapani, where they had claimed several B-17s attacking the nearby Sicilian port of Palermo. But this first spell of duty as a specialised bomber-destroyer unit was not to last long.

The Anglo-American invasion of Sicily on 10 July 1943 heralded a hasty return to the close-support role. For two weeks III./ZG 26 flew fighter-bomber and ground-attack missions as the invading Allies advanced across the island towards the Straits of Messina. It did not witness the fall of Sicily, however, for the *Gruppe* was ordered back to Germany before the end of July, thus finally bringing to an end more than 30 months of service in the Mediterranean.

The disappearance of III. *Gruppe* was not quite the final curtain, however. The semi-autonomous 10./ZG 26, formed back in April 1942 on Do 17s and since re-equipped with Ju 88s, would remain in south-east Europe until the coming autumn, flying ground-support missions during the German invasion of the Dodecanese Islands in September 1943.

One generally unremarked consequence of III./ZG 26's lengthy, somewhat isolated, and presumably valuable, period of operations in the Mediterranean is that it preserved the *Gruppe* from sharing the fate of every other *Zerstörer* unit – that of being swallowed up by either the ground-attack or nightfighter arms. In fact, III./ZG 26 was the *only* *Gruppe* to retain its *Zerstörer* designation throughout the convoluted history of the *Zerstörerwaffe*.

It thus became the one *Gruppe* to bridge the gap between the final

When 10./ZG 26 was withdrawn to form the 'new' 7./ZG 76 in October 1943, its place in the eastern Mediterranean was taken by the Ju 88-equipped 11./ZG 26. Here, '3U+KV' leads the *Staffel* as it takes off to support German paratroops on the Dodecanese island of Leros in November 1943. These aircraft also wear the *'Horst Wessel' Geschwader* badge, albeit in miniature form, together with the white silhouette of a diving eagle, the emblem of the Luftwaffe's paratroops

Bf 110s of II./ZG 1, recently withdrawn from the Russian Front, provided eleventh hour reinforcement for the beleaguered III./ZG 26 in the Mediterranean. For several weeks aircraft such as this 5. *Staffel* machine flew Ju 52 escort missions to and from Tunisia, as well as anti-bomber sorties over southern and central Italy – both to little effect

If II. *Gruppe*'s Bf 110s achieved minimal results, III./ZG 1's brief flirtation with the Me 210 was a disaster. Intended as the Bf 110's replacement, the Me 210 proved totally unacceptable. After flying Bf 109 fighter-bombers at El Alamein, III. *Gruppe* nevertheless converted to the Me 210 in Sicily shortly thereafter. Here, they are being prepared for a mission across the Sicilian Narrows to Tunisia

'2N+CD' of the *Gruppenstab* III./ZG 1 flies low over the Tunisian coastal plain, home to the *Gruppe* early in 1943. Note the 'Clog' emblem on the starboard nacelle, last seen on the Bf 110s of Hauptmann von Rettberg's II./ZG 26 in France in 1940

disappearance of the original pre-war *Zerstörer* force (whose otherwise last two *Gruppen* succumbed to the *Nachtjagdwaffe* in April 1942) and the re-creation of the 'new' *Zerstörergeschwader* of the mid-war years. In contrast to the early *Zerstörer*, whose intended role had been that of long-range air superiority (at which they failed so signally), but who found themselves increasingly employed as ground-attack aircraft, these second generation *Zerstörergeschwader* – the first two of which, ZGs 1 and 2, were activated as part of the preparations for the Eastern Front summer offensive of 1942 – were primarily fighter-bomber units.

Later released from the Russian front, two of the 'new' *Gruppen* – II.

Oberleutnant Heisel (kneeling left, bareheaded), *Staffelkapitän* of 2./ZG 26, briefs his crews prior to another mission at the start of Operation *Barbarossa*

Flying '3U+KK', Oberleutnant Heisel leads his *Staffel* at low-level over Wilno, a town in north-eastern Poland, and part of the territory occupied by the Russians in September 1939. Unfortunately, it is impossible to tell from the original print whether the white marks above the swastika on Heisel's aircraft are victory bars or a *Werk Nummer*

and III./ZG 1 – were transferred to the Mediterranean to participate in the closing stages of the African campaign and the defence of Sicily and Italy. But their hitherto predominantly ground-support experience, plus the strength of the Anglo-American opposition, prevented them from scoring all but a handful of aerial victories, and almost certainly precluded the emergence of any fresh *Experten*.

THE EASTERN FRONT

After playing their part in the Balkan and Cretan campaigns, I. and II./ZG 26 had returned briefly to the Homeland, before staging eastwards to Suwalki, in German-occupied Poland, in readiness for the invasion of the Soviet Union. Although the Luftwaffe had amassed more than 2500 frontline aircraft for the coming assault, Oberstleutnant Schalk's 51 serviceable Bf 110s provided the sole *Zerstörer* presence at the launch of Operation *Barbarossa*. Representing just two per cent of the total aerial armada, nothing better illustrates the sad decline of Göring's once seemingly invincible 'Ironsides'.

Although larger in scale than any campaign heretofore, *Barbarossa* opened in standard *Blitzkrieg* manner with the Luftwaffe attempting to neutralise enemy air opposition by simultaneous surprise attacks on Soviet airfields and landing grounds. By the end of the first day it is estimated that close on 1500 machines of the Red Air Force had been destroyed on the ground. The Bf 110s of ZG 26 took their toll in these opening rounds, but unlike the pilots of the single-engined *Jagdgeschwader* (many of whom now began to amass impressive scores), the *Zerstörer* crews found little aerial opposition, leaving this anonymous pilot to complain;

'The Russians won a battle without it even taking place. They brought

Bf 110 *ZERSTÖRER* UNITS ON THE EASTERN FRONT, 22 JUNE 1941

Luftflottenkommando 2 HQ: Warsaw

		Base	Type	Est-Serv
VIII. Fliegerkorps (Suwalki/Poland)				
Stab ZG 26	Oberstlt Johann Schalk	Suwalki	Bf 110C/E	4-4
I./ZG 26	Hpt Herbert Kaminski (Acting)	Suwalki	Bf 110C/E	38-17
II./ZG 26	Hpt Ralph von Rettberg	Suwalki	Bf 110C/E	36-30

Hauptmann Theodor Rossiwall, *Staffelkapitän* of 5./ZG 26, receives his Knight's Cross from General-oberst Albert Keller, C-in-C *Luftflottenkommando 1*, 6 August 1941

The photographer chose his moment with care before capturing this shot of a *Zerstörer* of II./ZG 26 – and its reflection – coming in to land at a waterlogged forward landing strip, which it is sharing with the Bf 109Fs of II./JG 54, on the road to Leningrad in the early autumn of 1941

the war down to ground level. They didn't like altitude – anything over 3000 metres they simply ignored.

'That, in turn, didn't suit us. It was only from 5000 (metres) upwards that our machines were able to show what they could really do. But the so-and-so's wouldn't play. They buzzed around in the lower regions attacking our ground troops, and didn't give a damn what was happening above them. This was all very well for our *Kampfgruppen*, who were going about their business completely undisturbed. But the infantry were sending up howls of protest and asking for help.

'Some bright spark back in Berlin had "discovered" that the best way to tackle a *Rata* (I-16) was from below. But how do you get underneath a machine that's flying ten metres above the ground? We couldn't dive on them either, for then we were simply shooting up our own troops below them. And from the sides the damn things seemed to be armoured like tortoises!

'So there was no other option but to attack them on their home bases. We were back to where we had left off in Crete. But with one big difference. There, we had found nothing. Here they were lined up in neat rows in front of their hangars. You could see their propeller discs shimmering in the sunlight from miles away – they made ideal targets.

'But do you think the things would burn? Not a chance. Two or three passes firing with everything you've got, then look back and what did you see? Forty or so machines still parked as if on parade, with perhaps one or two on fire – no more.

'Not even small bombs helped. A few aircraft might tip over and point a wing at the sky, but that was all. And the next morning, when you went through the whole performance for a second time, there they would be all standing upright again!'

By force of circumstance, the *Zerstörer* thus found themselves once more engaged primarily in ground-attack operations. From their jumping-off point on the central sector of the front, I. and II./ZG

26 were soon transferred northwards to support the German advance through the Baltic States towards Leningrad. To cover as much territory as possible, the *Gruppen*'s aircraft usually flew in individual pairs, or *Rotten*, keeping just within visual range of each other.

On the ground, too, their machines were often widely dispersed against possible counter-attack. For example, when they moved forward from Pleskau (Pskov) to Sarodinye, some 100 km to the east of Lake Peipus, one pilot noted in the squadron diary;

'Quite where or what Sarodinye actually was we never did discover. There was no town nearby, not even a village, just a spot in the middle of a forest. But it wasn't a bad airfield. In fact, it wasn't an airfield at all – just a lot of firebreaks cut among the trees. Each *Rotte* had its own runway, pointing in all directions. In the middle of it all a small clearing, surrounded by tall trees, where we set up our tents.'

By late August 1941 the Wehrmacht was within 50 km of Leningrad. For the *Zerstörer*, after more than two months of ground-support operations, attacking enemy infantry and supply columns, tanks and trains, airfields and forward landing strips, the war suddenly took a new turn, as another anonymous pilot noted;

'It was just like London and the south of England all over again. The flak around Leningrad was horrendous. We could understand now why the anti-aircraft defences of the many airfields we had encountered en route had been practically non-existent.

'Enemy fighters began to appear as well – something we hadn't experienced since leaving White Russia. Here, there were whole bunches of them, often flying at an altitude of 6000-7000 metres. But they weren't particularly dangerous. We could easily outmanoeuvre them. They occasionally tried to attack us, but clumsily and without skill. Our fighters (Bf 109s of JG 54) usually made short work of them.'

Part of the Luftwaffe force engaged against Leningrad during the winter of 1941-42, this all-white machine of ZG 26 can at least enjoy the 'benefits' of one of the established Soviet airfields in the area – possibly Siverskaya

The two *Zerstörergruppen* remained in the Leningrad area for several months, one of their principal tasks being the disruption of Soviet rail and river traffic in the region. During the winter of 1941-42, the *Staffeln* were rotated back to Germany to rest and refit. By the spring several had returned to the central sector of the Eastern Front, flying operations around Smolensk and Vitebsk. But moves were already underway to implement their long-postponed incorporation into the nightfighter arm. Before the end of April 1942, I. and II./ZG 26 had both disappeared from the Luftwaffe's frontline order of battle as the crews underwent training for their new role in the nocturnal defence of the Reich as I. and II./NJG 4.

The ten months spent in the Soviet Union had enabled many ZG 26 pilots to amass a considerable tally of ground successes. And, despite the apparent dearth of aerial opposition for much of the period, a number of *Experten* had also managed to add to their personal scores of enemy aircraft shot down. During this time some half-dozen Knight's Crosses were presented to members of the two *Gruppen*.

From close-up, the temporary white winter camouflage applied to the *Geschwader*'s Bf 110s does not appear quite so pristine. Muffled up against the winter cold, Oberfeldwebel Herbert Schob proudly surveys his double-figure scoreboard. Of the ten kills shown, nine had been claimed prior to *Barbarossa*. Only the tenth, it is believed, indicates a Soviet victim. Note the initials below the cockpit of Wk-Nr 3901

Major Wilhelm Spies, *Gruppenkommandeur* of I./ZG 26, achieved 11 aerial victories in the east. Pictured here wearing the Knight's Cross awarded on 14 June 1941, Spies was honoured with posthumous Oak Leaves after being killed in action on 27 January 1942

The winter of 1941 seems to have caught up with the rear half of this Bf 110C of II./SKG 210, or is it just that the forward areas of temporary winter white have been all but worn away? Note that no attempt has been made to cover the elaborate 'Wasp' nose marking

The first pair, awarded a week prior to the launch of *Barbarossa*, had been for the recipients' recent activities in the Balkans, one going to Hauptmann Wilhelm Spies, erstwhile *Staffelkapitän* of 1./ZG 26, for ten victories, and the other to Hauptmann Ralph von Rettberg, long-serving *Gruppenkommandeur* of II./ZG 26 with four kills, in recognition of his outstanding leadership. On 6 August 1941 two more Hauptleute and unit COs were similarly honoured, with Theodor Rossiwall (5./ZG 26) having also scored ten kills and Herbert Kaminski (I./ZG 26) claiming five.

On 10 October II./ZG 26's Oberleutnant Werner Thierfelder had received the Knight's Cross when his score was standing at 14. But it was the last two decorations awarded during the *Gruppen*'s service in Russia which most clearly illustrate the type of operations they had been flying of late. Leutnant Eduard Meyer's Knight's Cross, presented on 20 December, was for 18 aerial victories plus 48 aircraft (and two tanks) destroyed on the ground. And Oberleutnant Johannes Kiel's award, dated 18 March 1942, was even more indicative. In addition to 20 aircraft shot down, he had destroyed a further 62 on the ground, plus nine tanks and 20 artillery pieces, as well as sinking one submarine, three MTBs and a transport vessel!

Such successes did not come cheaply, however. And among the many casualties sustained in the Soviet Union were two of the above Knight's Cross holders. On 27 January 1942 Major Wilhelm Spies, by now *Gruppenkommandeur* of I./ZG 26 and with 20 kills to his credit, had been shot down during a close-support mission near Sukhinichi. Spies, who had flown with the *Condor Legion* in Spain, was the first member of the original *Zerstörerwaffe* to be awarded the Oak Leaves (albeit posthumously, on 5 April 1942). The other Knight's Cross recipient to be lost was Leutnant Eduard Meyer, whose Bf 110 was involved in a mid-air collision while flying a ground-attack operation near Velizh on 31 March 1942 – only days prior to ZG 26's withdrawal from the Eastern Front.

Back at the start of Operation *Barbarossa*, there had, in fact, been two other Bf 110-equipped *Gruppen* assigned to *Luftflotte 2* on the central sector. These were I. and II./*Schnellkampfgeschwader* 210 (the original *Erprobungsgruppe* 210 of the Battle of Britain, and the erstwhile III./ZG 76 respectively). As their current designation suggests, these units were,

however, dedicated 'fast bomber' *Gruppen*, their role being exclusively ground-support.

Such operations, which usually consisted of first dive-bombing the assigned target and then following up with cannon-strafing, involved the two *Gruppen* in the great cauldron battles of the central sector as they followed the ground forces advancing on Moscow. Within two months they had moved forward to Vitebsk, and by the year's end had reached Orel and Bryansk, some 350 km to the south-west of the Soviet capital. The *Schnellkampf* pilots did not necessarily seek air combat, especially when laden with bombs, but neither did they go out of their way to avoid it. A number of aerial engagements occurred on the road to Moscow, but these were usually more by accident than design, and often proved inconclusive, as one pilot supporting German Panzers in an armoured clash near Senno recalls;

In this close-up of armourers attaching bombs to the ventral rack of a Bf 110, it is clear that the wasp emblem has been deliberately left intact, with the white winter camouflage only being applied from a point roughly level with the windscreen

Although chronologically out of order, this similar close-up of a Me 410 is included to illustrate the same emblem (now of II./ZG 1), but much reduced in size. It also serves to demonstrate the *Gruppe's* changing role, the close-support bomb rack of 1941 giving way to the anti-bomber ventral gun pack of 1944. Note also the non-retractable handgrip below the cockpit of the Me 410 and the fighter-style spinner spiral

'Suddenly, out of the blue, we were attacked by a whole squadron of Russian fighters. Taken completely by surprise, I was hit several times and once again had to make my way back to base on one engine. I did manage to get a couple of shots of my own in, but didn't witness the result as he immediately sheered off and I had my hands full trying to feather my overheating engine.'

There were nevertheless two Knight's Crosses won during these stages of the advance. Both were awarded to members of II./SKG 210 on 5 October 1941, with one going to veteran NCO pilot Oberfeldwebel Johannes Lutter, whose score at the time was standing at seven aerial kills, plus a further 30 enemy aircraft destroyed on the ground, together with 15 tanks knocked out, and the other to 13-victory *Experte* Oberleutnant Günther Tonne.

Early in 1942 the rather cumbersome *'Schnellkampf'* designation was discarded in favour of a return to the more familiar *'Zerstörer'*.

I. and II./SKG 210 now became I. and II./ZG 1 (a III. *Gruppe* was created from scratch and equipped with Bf 109s and, later, the Me 210). Despite the reversion to the earlier title, the *Gruppen's* tasks remained the same. The only thing to change was ZG 1's axis of advance, for Moscow was no longer the goal. The 1942 offensive would be launched along the southern sector, the objective – Stalingrad.

The year started badly for II./ZG 1. On 3 February they lost their long-serving *Kommandeur* when Hauptmann Rolf Kaldrack's Bf 110 was brought down near Toropez after being rammed by a crashing MiG-1 fighter. Kaldrack, who rejoiced in the nickname of 'Schlitzohr' (literally 'Slit ear', but meaning something along the lines of 'Artful dodger'), had taken over the *Gruppe* during its time as III./ZG 76 at the height of the Battle of Britain. He had been awarded the Knight's Cross at the close of that historic conflict and now, six days after his death, was honoured with posthumous Oak Leaves. The latter decoration was not so much for his ten Eastern Front aerial victories as for his inspired leadership during the *Gruppe's* recent 'fast bomber' operations during the advance on Moscow.

Throughout 1942, ZG 1 supported Army Group South as it advanced across the Ukraine and into the Caucasus. They dive-bombed Soviet artillery positions and flew long-range missions against the enemy's road and rail lines of supply and reinforcement. By the summer, they were operating in the Rostov region and over the Sea of Azov. Aerial opposition was still a matter of chance, something to be dealt with as and when it occurred. During one dive-bombing mission against gun placements along the River Donets, for example;

'Quite unexpectedly, the Soviet air force turned up. A *Pulk* of about 15 to 20 I-153s attacked us. These manoeuvrable little biplanes were very hard to catch, as our Bf 110s were too unwieldy for that kind of job. Although on this occasion I did succeed in shooting one down – more by luck than judgement, it must be said. I almost rammed him from behind, and to this day I don't know where he appeared from. The rough and tumble didn't last long. The enemy disappeared as suddenly as he had arrived.'

After operations over the Kerch peninsula, ZG 1 moved up into the Don Bend, following 6. *Armee* as it pushed towards Stalingrad. By August they were based at Armavir and Frolov. From here they mounted strikes against enemy rail traffic in and around Stalin's showpiece city on the Volga. As Soviet resistance hardened, they were employed increasingly in the anti-tank role, dive-bombing and strafing Russian armour, each crew often flying four or five sorties a day. For the first time they began to carry 1000-kg bombs (double their usual load), and although the surface of the steppe airfields were baked stone hard by the August sun, they were not particularly even. Great care had to be exercised on take-off. Attacks had to be right first time, too, for there was no going round for a second attempt. Pulling out of a 70° dive with a 1000-kg bomb under the belly was liable to tear the wings right off a Bf 110!

The three Knight's Crosses awarded to the *Geschwader* over the next three months testified yet again to the continuing dominance of their ground-support activities. Leutnant Herbert Kutscha of II./ZG 1 – the first to be decorated (on 24 September) – scored 14 aerial victories in the east. But his list of ground successes is even more impressive, for he is credited with the destruction of 44 aircraft, 41 tanks, 15 locomotives, 11 artillery pieces and 157 trucks! I. *Gruppe*'s Leutnant Rudolf Scheffel, who received his Knight's Cross on 29 October, claimed just five aerial kills, but was credited with the destruction of ten times that number of tanks. And on 25 November II./ZG 1's Oberfeldwebel Hans Peterburs was awarded the decoration for 18 enemy aircraft shot down, plus another 26 (and 19 tanks) destroyed on the ground.

Operations of such a nature and such a scale were bound to take a heavy toll. The losses suffered by von Paulus' 6. *Armee* at Stalingrad are well known, and ZG 1's casualties were proportionately just as grievous. By year-end, the two *Gruppen* could muster but a handful of serviceable Bf 110s between them. But still they were thrown into the battle. Reprieve did not come until 28 January 1943. On that date, six Bf 109s and five Bf 110s – the only aircraft available – were scheduled to fly long-range fighter patrols over the beleaguered city. But Major Wilcke, *Geschwaderkommodore* of JG 3, who was co-ordinating fighter operations, demurred. The *Zerstörer*, he protested, were simply not suitable for such a task. He was overruled by no lesser an individual thanGeneralfeldmarschall Erhard Milch;

'I will brook no opposition. The credibility of the Luftwaffe, and the fighters in particular, is on the line.'

The mission was flown as ordered and the *Zerstörer* suffered the inevitable losses.

Three days later ZG 1's ten serviceable Bf 110s turned their backs on Stalingrad. They retired to Rostov and Novocherkassk, some 320 km to the west. Although new crews and aircraft arrived to make good the attrition suffered, the *Geschwader*'s days in Russia were numbered. In March 1943 II./ZG 1 was withdrawn to the Reich, before being sent to the Mediterranean – III./ZG 1 had been transferred from the Eastern Front to North Africa the previous autumn.

I. *Gruppe* remained in the east for another four months. Redeployed to the central sector of the front in May 1943, their tank-busting career in Russia culminated in their participating in the greatest armoured clash in history – the Battle of Kursk. But 17 bomb-carrying Bf 110s could do little to influence the outcome of this titanic struggle, and by the end of July 1943 I./ZG 1, too, had returned to Germany, where they would be duly redesignated to become the new I./ZG 26.

One remnant of ZG 1 remained in Russia for a few weeks longer, however. Back in September 1942, the *Geschwader* had set up a provisional nightfighter *Staffel*, although 10.(NJ)/ZG 1's strength had rarely reached double figures. For much of its brief history it could field only three or four serviceable machines, yet this small unit produced one outstanding *Experte*. Josef Kociok had joined III./ZG 76 in 1940. During this *Gruppe*'s time as

Eastern front nightfighter *Experte*, Oberfeldwebel Josef Kociok (left), uses his 'victory stick' to point at his scoreboard, which is currently standing at 12 day kills and 8 night. A further 7 nocturnal victories would earn Kociok the Knight's Cross

II./SKG 210, Kociok had excelled as a ground-support pilot, claiming 15 aircraft destroyed on the ground, plus four tanks and over 200 vehicles. He also achieved a dozen aerial kills. It is uncertain exactly when he transferred to 10.(NJ)/ZG 1, but he rose to even greater heights as a nightfighter. Oberfeldwebel Kociok was awarded the Knight's Cross on 31 July 1943, and he remained with the unit after its redesignation as the *Nachtjagdschwarm/Luftflotte 4* the following month. He was finally killed over the Kerch Peninsula on 26 September when his Bf 110 was struck by a crashing Soviet fighter. Posthumously promoted to Leutnant, Josef Kociok had scored 21 nocturnal victories.

But even this was not quite the end of the *Zerstörer* in the east. While the original ZG 26 and SKG 210 (aka ZG 1) had been active on the main sectors of the front, another semi-autonomous *Zerstörerstaffel* had been operating in the far north, astride and above the Arctic Circle.

This unit's origins dated back to early 1941 when the Norwegian-based JG 77 had established a Bf 110 *Zerstörerkette* (unit of three aircraft) for coastal patrol purposes. By the beginning of *Barbarossa*, the *Kette* had been expanded to *Staffel* strength. Based at Kirkenes, in northern Norway, under the command of Oberleutnant Felix Maria Brandis, 1.(Z)/JG 77 initially flew bomber-escort missions against the Russian port of Murmansk, and its surrounding airfields. Despite the remote and barren nature of its area of operations – and the fact that it, too, was also to be employed for much of the time on ground-support and attack missions – the *Staffel* produced a clutch of *Experten*.

The first of these was not, strictly speaking, a member of the *Staffel*, but the *Führer* of the temporarily attached *Stabsschwarm* ZG 76. Hauptmann Gerhard Schaschke racked up a considerable score during the opening weeks of the campaign in the east. Using a tactic of his own devising (escorted by a high-flying Bf 109, Schaschke would overfly a Soviet airfield, apparently alone, and then dive on the Russian fighters invariably sent up to engage him), his tally soon reached double figures. But it was a dangerous ploy, and on 4 August 1941, by which time he had 20 enemy aircraft to his credit, Schaschke's Bf 110 was brought down by AA fire. He survived to be taken prisoner, but subsequently disappeared while in Soviet captivity.

Another Arctic *Zerstörer* ace was 1.(Z)/JG 77's first *Staffelkapitän*, Oberleutnant Brandis, whose score stood at 14 when he was killed in a

On the Arctic front in the winter of 1941-42, Oberleutnant Felix Maria Brandis (right), *Staffelkapitän* of 1.(Z)/JG 77, and Feldwebel Baus admire the evidence of their combined handiwork – 14 Soviet aircraft brought down. There would be no more kills, however, for this crew failed to return from a sortie south of Murmansk on 2 February 1942

After JG 77's withdrawal from the region, the Arctic *Zerstörerstaffel* was redesignated, in turn, as 6., 10. and, finally, 13.(Z)/JG 5. This Bf 110G, '1B+AX' (Wk-Nr 120037), is of the *Staffel*. Pictured in the winter of 1943-44, it is probably the aircraft of the then *Staffelkapitän,* Hauptmann Herbert Treppe (3 victories)

crash on 2 February 1942. Returning at low level from a train-busting mission along the railway line south of Murmansk, the *Staffel* suddenly flew into a bad-weather front. With their own base closed in, the Bf 110s were ordered to divert to Rovaniemi. In zero visibility, flying low over a featureless landscape of frozen lakes, three aircraft – including that piloted by Brandis – failed to make it.

Brandis' successor, Oberleutnant Karl-Fritz Schlosstein, was to remain at the head of the *Staffel* until the summer of 1943. During that period the unit underwent several redesignations (occasioned by the parent *Geschwader*, JG 77, being replaced on the Arctic Front by JG 5), while Schlosstein's personal score rose to eight.

But the most successful of all *Zerstörer* pilots in the far north was a 26-year-old NCO straight out of training school. Feldwebel Theodor Weissenberger had joined 1.(Z)/JG 77 at Kirkenes on 14 September 1941. He claimed his first victory, an I-153, on 24 October, and by the time he was posted to II./JG 5, and single-seaters, in September 1942, Weissenberger had scored no fewer than 23 kills, including eight Hurricanes.

Latterly as 13.(Z)/JG 5, the *Staffel* continued to fight on over the Arctic until finally being withdrawn from Finland in February 1944. It then spent several months back where it had started, patrolling the Norwegian seaboard, before being incorporated into the new IV./ZG 26 as that *Gruppe's* 10. *Staffel*.

THE WESTERN FRONT

The severe attrition suffered by the *Zerstörerwaffe* during the Battle of Britain had effectively written *finis* to the Bf 110 as a viable daylight combat aircraft in north-west Europe. With but a few minor exceptions, the most notable, perhaps, being II./ZG 76's brief deployment along the North Sea coast during the latter half of 1941 (after the *Gruppe's* return from Crete and before its redesignation as III./NJG 3), the Bf 110 *Zerstörer* was to play no further part in the escalating air war over occupied Western Europe.

There is, however, one *Gruppe* which does deserve mention in the context of western-based *Zerstörer Experten*. Just as KG 30 had established a

The crew of U-515 obviously appreciate I./ZG 1's services in safeguarding their passage across the Bay of Biscay. At the time the photograph was taken (9 November 1943), this highly successful boat had already sunk 24 Allied ships, and five more would be claimed before the year was out. But then U-515 would herself be sent to the bottom by US Navy carrier aircraft north of Madeira on 9 April 1944

subordinate Ju 88 *Zerstörer* component during the Norwegian campaign, so too, in the autumn of 1942, did KG 40 (the long-range bomber unit whose Fw 200s had been dubbed the 'Scourge of the Atlantic' by no less a personage than Prime Minister Winston Churchill) deploy its own *Gruppe* of Ju 88 *Zerstörer* in western France.

V./KG 40's primary task was not to escort its parent *Geschwader*'s bombers, but rather to safeguard Admiral Doenitz's U-Boats during their hazardous passage across the Bay of Biscay to and from their hunting

The Ju 88 in the foreground ('F8+RY' of 14./KG 40) illustrates the new overwater camouflage scheme being introduced by the *Gruppe* for Biscay operations

This in-flight shot of a 14. *Staffel Schwarm* shows the new two-tone(?) camouflage scheme even more clearly. Note, too, the elaborate spinner markings

A representative quartet of Biscay *Zerstörer* victims brought down in 1943: US Navy PBY Catalina of VP-63 on 1 August (right); a Mosquito FB IV of No 192 ECM Sqn on 11 August (far right); a No 461 Sqn Sunderland III on 16 September (bottom right); and a Horsa glider towed by a No 295 Sqn Halifax V on 18 September (bottom far right)

grounds in the Atlantic. The *Gruppe* also preyed upon Allied air traffic, skirting the Bay en route from the UK to Gibraltar and the Mediterranean.

Faced with a wealth of targets ranging from the formidable anti-submarine Sunderlands of Coastal Command – known to the Luftwaffe as 'Flying Porcupines' on account of their heavy defensive armament – to the near-defenceless glider-tug combinations being despatched across the Bay to North Africa in preparation for the airborne invasion of Sicily, the *Gruppe* claimed some 80 victories during its first year of operations. At least three pilots, Oberleutnant Hermann Horstmann, Dieter Meister and Kurt Necesany, also achieved five kills apiece.

Thus, when V./KG 40 was redesignated I./ZG 1 (the third such!) in October 1943, it had a ready-made trio of *Experten*, each of whom subsequently added a sixth victory while flying as *bona fide Zerstörer* pilots. A fourth member of V./KG 40, Oberleutnant Albrecht Bellstedt, had scored four kills (one being a civilian DC-3 airliner, whose passengers included the celebrated British film actor Leslie Howard, star of *First of the Few*). Appointed *Staffelkapitän* of 2./ZG 1 on 8 November 1943, Bellstedt achieved ace status 48 hours later when he brought down a No 228 Sqn Sunderland off northern Spain's Cape Ortegal.

The attrition was not all one-sided, however. This damaged Ju 88, desperately dumping fuel, will be lucky to make it back to base on the one engine . . .

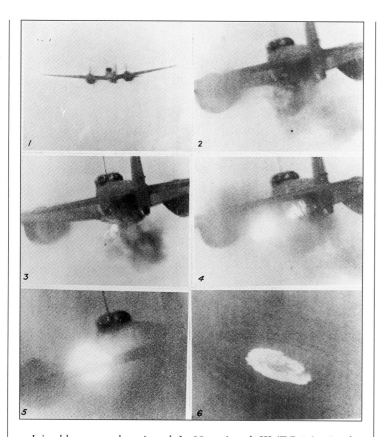

Two of the Biscay *Experten* – Oberleutnant Hermann Horstmann (centre) and Leutnant Dieter Meister (right) are seen with Leutnant Barzel in front of a Ju 88R. Horstmann, *Staffelkapitän* of 1./ZG 1, was killed in action against Beaufighters on 12 December 1943. Dieter Meister converted to single-seaters and lost his life flying an Fw 190 as *Staffelkapitän* of 10./JG 2 on 21 November 1944

Joined by a recently activated, Ju 88-equipped, III./ZG 1 (again, the third unit to be so designated!) in the winter of 1943-44, the *Gruppe* remained on the Biscay coast until the Allied invasion of Normandy in June 1944. Thrown into action against the beachheads, the two *Gruppen* sustained such grievous losses that they were disbanded soon afterwards. The surviving pilots were then incorporated into the *Jagdwaffe*, the majority providing the nuclei of the new II. and III./JG 4.

Of the four *Experten* mentioned above, two had already been posted missing during operations with I./ZG 1. The remaining pair, Oberleutnants Bellstedt and Meister, were both killed before the end of 1944 while serving in defence of the Homeland as the *Staffelkapitäne* of 9. and 10./JG 2 respectively.

DEFENCE OF THE REICH

The obvious shortcomings of the original *Zerstörergruppen* had led to many of them being gainfully re-employed as nightfighters – a task they would perform valiantly until the end of the war. The second-generation *Zerstörer* units were also offered the chance of a new lease of life. Initially formed in 1942 primarily for low-level ground-support duties on the Eastern Front, they were now to be retrained as high-altitude daylight bomber destroyers in Defence of the Reich.

On paper it was not an unsound proposal. The Bf 110 provided a solid and steady weapons platform. It could carry heavy, hard-hitting armament, including 5 cm cannon and rocket launchers, and had sufficient range to stalk an enemy bomber formation while waiting for an oppor-

A

B

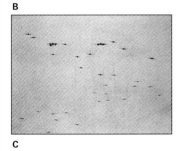

C

An early Defence of the Reich operation unfolds as (A) the *Zerstörer* keep well off the starboard beam of the US bomber box while waiting for the fighter escort to turn back. (B) The Bf 110s now curve in towards the 'heavies', (C) closing in on them from the rear. Underwing rockets are launched (D), and explosions darken the sky (E) as one B-17 (centre far left) lurches out of formation trailing smoke. Finally, a 1st Division Fortress (F) starts to go down

But with the advent of longer-range escort fighters – here a P-47 Thunderbolt, but more particularly the P-51 Mustang – the *Zerstörer* crews all too soon found their roles reversed. They were no longer the hunters, but the hunted

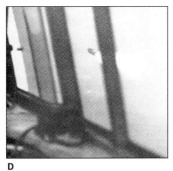

D

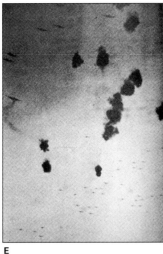

E

F

tune moment to attack. What the planners failed to take into account was that the added weaponry would render the unwieldy Bf 110 even more vulnerable to Allied fighters.

At first this did not pose too big a problem. The *Zerstörer* could bide their time until the short-legged escorts were forced to turn back before attacking the Eighth AF's heavy bombers. They could then act as true *Pulk-Zerstörer* (literally 'breakers-up of formations') by lobbing heavy cannon shells and rockets at the bomber boxes, often disrupting their rigid formations and allowing the single-engined Bf 109s and Fw 190s to get in amongst them. Although not without danger from the massed return fire of the bombers' heavy machine-guns, it was during this period that most of the *Zerstörers'* successes against the *Viermots* were achieved.

But the arrival upon the scene of the long-range P-51 Mustang in late December 1943 altered everything. The Eighth's 'heavies' were soon enjoying the benefit of fighter escort into the furthermost corners of the Reich and back. The *Zerstörer* had nowhere to hide, and their losses spiralled alarmingly. A last-ditch attempt to redress the balance by re-equipping the *Zerstörergruppen* with Me 410s in the spring of 1944 simply postponed the inevitable. At another time and in another environment the Me 410 could have been a useful aircraft. But in the

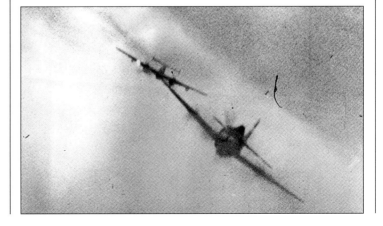

skies over Germany in the summer of 1944 it was as outclassed as the Bf 110 had been over southern England four years earlier. Within weeks the first Me 410 *Gruppen* were being disbanded, and before the year was out the *Zerstörerwaffe* had ceased to exist.

The first move towards introducing the Bf 110 into the daylight Defence of the Reich had been the transferring of I./ZG 1 from Orel, in Russia, to Wunstorf, near Hannover, in July 1943. An anonymous pilot assigned to the *Gruppe* at the time remembers;

'Each *Staffel*'s losses were made good by intakes from the *Ergänzungsgruppen* and trainees straight out of flying school. We began to practise the new tactics to be employed against the "dicke Autos" ("fat cars" – heavy bombers). We also got four *"Dödels"* (rocket tubes) to hang under our wings. We shot off some live rounds over the German Bight. It was quite a fireworks display when all four were fired together in one salvo. It felt as if the old crate was going to fly apart at the seams!'

At Wunstorf the veteran Eastern Front crews were broken up, with experienced pilots being paired with a new rear-seat crewman, and vice-versa – this was viewed as the best way to assimilate the tyros, and prepare them for the task ahead. III./ZG 1 underwent the same process, having likewise returned to the Reich for retraining from central Italy, exchanging their near useless Me 210s for the improved Me 410. By mid-October 1943, with their training and working-up completed, the two *Gruppen* were re-designated to become the 'new' I. and II./ZG 26 respectively (their previous ZG 1 identities now being assumed by the two Biscay-based Ju 88 *Gruppen*).

II./ZG 1 had also been withdrawn from Italy (in July) – not back to the Reich, but to the French Atlantic coast. Based first at Lorient, and then at Brest-South, their Bf 110s had operated over the Bay of Biscay alongside V./KG 40's Ju 88s. They achieved little, however, and suffered the loss of their *Gruppenkommandeur* when Hauptmann Karl-Heinrich Matern was shot down off Brest by Australian Spitfires on 8 October. Matern was awarded a posthumous Knight's Cross the following day, mainly on the strength of his earlier ground-support activities on the Eastern Front, where most, if not all, of his 12 aerial victories had also been scored.

Later in October 1943, II./ZG 1 was transferred to Wels, in Austria. Here, they would remain until the

Despite the recent advent of Allied escort fighters, the crew of this cannon- and rocket-armed Bf 110G of the 'new' ZG 26 seem remarkably unconcerned. One man sits on the windscreen frame reading a book, while the other relaxes on the wing. Even the attendant groundcrew member appears to have nodded off on the ground below. Maybe this shot was taken at a training field (note the Luftwaffe-coded glider in the background, left), or could it possibly have been posed?

A fully-loaded *Pulk-Zerstörer* of II./ZG 1 patrols the Austrian Alps

Photographed against an inhospitable Alpine background from a US bomber, an unidentified Me 410 (left) can be seen chasing a lone B-24 after the bombing raid on Steyr, Austria, of 23 February 1944. This is no doubt the result of a *Herausschuss* (literally a 'shooting-out' – damaging a bomber sufficiently to force it to drop out of the mutually protective fire zone of its combat box so that it can then be picked off as a straggler)

following summer (with a month spent in Rumania) combating heavy bomber incursions from the south by the Italian-based US Fifteenth AF. Led by Hauptmann Egon Albrecht, whose Knight's Cross had been won on 25 May 1943 when his tally of victories include 15 aircraft shot down and another 11 destroyed on the ground in Russia, the *Gruppe* enjoyed some success over their new Alpine battleground. For example, on 2 April 1944, they claimed six 'heavies' destroyed during the Fifteenth's attacks on Steyr and Graz. But their casualties were mounting too. On 29 May they lost a dozen Bf 110s to American escort fighters south-east of Vienna without being able to bring down a single bomber.

Such losses could not be sustained for long. In July 1944 the *Gruppe* returned to Germany for conversion onto the Bf 109 and redesignation as III./JG 76. They were then despatched to the Western Front where, on

The yellow Eastern Front bands around the fuselages of both the late-production Me 323 six-engined transport and the cannon-equipped Bf 110G coming in to land above would suggest that this photograph was taken during II./ZG 1's brief sojourn at Mamaia, Rumania, in April 1944. Unfortunately, the small *Geschwader* code combination ahead of the fuselage cross on 'PN' is indecipherable

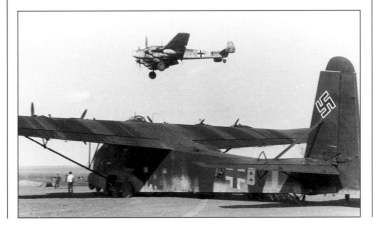

25 August – four days after their arrival – *Gruppenkommandeur* Egon Albrecht was shot down by Mustangs, his final score having risen in the interim to some 25 kills, including at least three *Viermots* downed over the Alps.

While II./ZG 1 had been defending the Reich's southern ramparts, the two-thirds 'new' ZG 26 had been facing the might of the Eighth AF in the north. Led at first by *Geschwaderkommodore* Ralph von Rettberg, I. and II./ZG 26 had been joined by the veteran III. *Gruppe* recently returned from their long odyssey in the Mediterranean. The latter found a very different war awaiting them in northern Germany.

A pattern of steady attrition was set right from the very start. One of ZG 26's earliest actions, against the major US raid on Münster of 10 October 1943, resulted in casualties among both II. and III. *Gruppen*. The *Zerstörer* struck back four days later during 'second Schweinfurt' when their rockets were responsible for bringing down several bombers. This initial success with *Zerstörer*-launched air-to-air rockets prompted Messerschmitt to design and install a six-barrel revolving launcher in the nose of a Me 410. Fired individually in quick succession, the resulting fusillade blew the nose panels off the aircraft!

ZG 26's problems really began with the advent of the Mustang. The American fighter flew its first long-range escort mission on 13 December

Toting underwing rockets, this Bf 110G ('3U+KR') of the ex-Mediterranean III./ZG 26 would discover a very different kind of war being waged in defence of the Reich

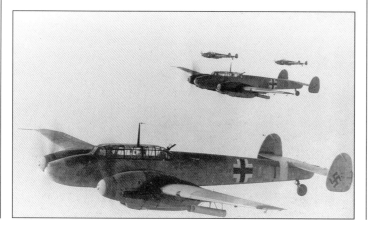

A *Schwarm* of 9./ZG 26 machines ('3U+DT' in the foreground) sets off to do battle with the US Eighth AF. Each aircraft is armed with four 210 mm underwing rockets and a ventral 30 mm cannon pack

The lead *Zerstörer* of this formation – reportedly of 4./ZG 76 up from Neubiberg near Munich on 13 January 1944 – is unmistakably equipped with the 37 mm BK 3,7 (*Flak* 18) cannon, one hit from which was usually sufficient to disable a B-17 Flying Fortress

1943 – a round trip to Kiel and back of almost 1000 miles (1600 km). And it was very likely a ZG 26 machine which provided the P-51 with its first kill of the conflict when the 354th FG's 1Lt Glenn T Eagleston (see *Osprey Aircraft of the Aces 7 - Mustang Aces of the Ninth and Fifteenth Air Forces and the RAF*) was credited with the probable destruction of a Bf 110 over Friedrichstadt at 1325 hrs on that date.

The *Geschwader*'s casualties escalated during the first quarter of 1944. On 20 February, during the USAAF's 'Big Week' campaign against German aircraft production centres, Major Johann Kogler's III./ZG 26 lost 11 out of 13 Bf 110s despatched against the 'heavies'. But the hardest individual blow occurred two days later when the Me 410 of Major Eduard Tratt, *Gruppenkommandeur* of II./ZG 26, was shot down over the Harz Mountains. Tratt had first joined the original I./ZG 1 early in 1940. He had been awarded the Knight's Cross on 12 April 1942 for achieving 20 aerial victories (including 12 over the Channel) and for his

A photograph probably taken at Königsberg in der Neumark during conversion training on the Me 410. Massed low-level flypasts such as this may have impressed the citizens of Berlin, but would have been God's gift to a band of marauding Mustangs

Major Johann Kogler, *Gruppenkommandeur* of III./ZG 26 during the early Defence of the Reich operations, was promoted to command of the *Geschwader* in May 1944. Remaining in office after the transition to JG 6, *Geschwaderkommodore* Oberstleutnant Johann Kogler was shot down and captured during Operation *Bodenplatte,* the *Jagdwaffe*'s last-ditch attack on Allied airfields on New Year's Day 1945

ground-support activities in Russia. Since then, he had scored another 18 kills. With a total of 38 enemy aircraft to his credit (including several *Viermots*), Eduard Tratt was, and would remain, the highest scoring *Zerstörer* pilot of the war.

On 6 March 1944 II. and III./ZG 26 lost another 11 aircraft of the 17 which attacked US heavy bombers targeting Berlin. It was clear that the *Geschwader* could not survive for long under such circumstances, for not only were the *Gruppen* suffering swingeing losses in the air, their aircraft were also being hit heavily on the ground by marauding Allied fighters. They were therefore withdrawn from their bases in north-west Germany and transferred to Königsberg in der Neumark (a small town some 90 km to the north-east of Berlin) before the end of March. Although by no means beyond the range of the ubiquitous Mustangs, here they were at least out of the immediate firing line of the incoming bomber streams.

At Königsberg I. and III. *Gruppen* began conversion to the Me 410. On quiet days, when no enemy bomber raids were reported approaching,

A *Schwarm* of II./ZG 76 prepares to take off. Although none of the aircraft carry underwing rocket launchers,the two furthermost machines are equipped with extended-barrel 20 mm MG 151 nose cannon

The extended-barrel MG 151 nose armament is shown more clearly in this informal ground shot. Note, too, the presentation of the *Geschwader* code (one-fifth of the original size by this stage of the war) and the spiralled spinners

These 1./ZG 76 machines are pictured returning in good order to Salzburg on 16 April 1944 – a day on which the US Fifteenth AF's 'heavies' struck at targets in Rumania and Yugoslavia

I. Jagd-Division HQ in Berlin-Döberitz would call upon the *Gruppen* to overfly the capital at low-level to boost civilian morale! Such occasions were rare, however, and losses would soon be climbing again. But before that a number of changes had taken place.

In May 1944 two *Staffeln* of Hauptmann Werner Thierfelder's III./ZG 26 had left the *Geschwader* to form a test unit equipped with Me 262 jets. Command of the truncated ZG 26 had now passed from Major Karl Boehm-Tettelbach to Major Johann Kogler. The latter could do little more than oversee the demise of his two Me 410-equipped *Gruppen*, and in just six of their many engagements over the course of the next eight

Hauptmann Johannes Kiel supervises the loading of 210 mm rockets into the underwing tubes on his aircraft. One of the 'Old Guard' of the *Zerstörerwaffe*, Kiel had assumed command of 7./ZG 26 in August 1943. He was promoted to *Gruppenkommandeur* II./ZG 76 in November, but was killed in action on 29 January 1944

weeks, I. and II./ZG 26 suffered the loss of 80 crew members killed or wounded. Bowing to the inevitable, the two *Zerstörergruppen* retired to East Prussia in August to convert on to the Fw 190 and re-form as JG 6.

The single-engined Fw 190 was no guarantee of survival, however, for Leutnant Rudi Dassow (who had been with II./ZG 26 since 1942, and was one of the most successful pilots flying in Defence of the Reich – 12 of his 22 victories being four-engined bombers) lost his life only days after conversion to the Focke-Wulf. He was shot down in flames near Laon, in France, on 25 August. Another ex-ZG 26 pilot with a dozen *Viermots* among his 17+ claims was Hauptmann Peter Jenne, who would be killed in action on 2 March 1945 while serving as *Staffelkapitän* of 12./JG 300.

The third, and final, *Zerstörergeschwader* to be embroiled in the daylight Defence of the Homeland was the 'new' ZG 76. Unlike the other two, this had no previous history, with its three component *Gruppen* being made up of a miscellany of other *Staffeln* (the majority of them came from the reconnaissance arm).

I. and II./ZG 76 were activated in August and September 1943 respectively, with command of the incomplete and largely untried *Geschwader* being given to the highly experienced Major Theodor Rossiwall. Moves to create a III. *Gruppe* were begun in November, and although it never reached full strength and was eventually disbanded again the following

Fitted with a 30 mm ventral cannon pack, and with the tips of the 210 mm rockets just visible in their underwing launch tubes, a fully-loaded *Pulk-Zerstörer* of Helmut Haugk's 4./ZG 76 ('2N+EM') climbs to meet the enemy

A photograph of indifferent quality, but some rarity, showing a mixed *Zerstörer* formation – the machine in the foreground is equipped with the lethal 37 mm *Flak* 18 cannon, whilst the Bf 110 behind it has a single 210 mm rocket under each wing. If this combination could get within striking distance of a heavy bomber formation (and, of the two, the latter would stand the better chance), it could inflict serious damage . . .

... but as the months passed, such chances grew ever slimmer. Although taken late in 1943, this sequence of shots – showing the destruction by a US fighter of the right-hand wingman of a *Schwarm* of rocket-carrying *Zerstörer* – graphically encapsulates the fate of the Bf 110 over Germany in 1944. It was simply blown out of the sky

spring, it was III./ZG 76 which lost one of the *Geschwader*'s few *Experten*. *Gruppenkommandeur* Hauptmann Johannes Kiel was shot down south-west of Mainz on 29 January 1944 during an engagement which netted ZG 76 three B-17s destroyed.

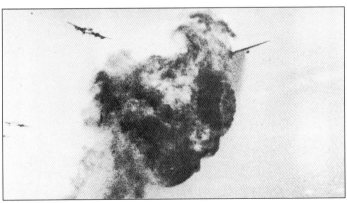

Attempts to re-equip the last of the *Zerstörergruppen* with Me 410s were short-lived

Such successes, however relatively minor, were the exception rather than the norm. The history of the second-generation ZG 76 in the Defence of Reich is again little more than a catalogue of steady losses – in the Berlin raid of 6 March 1944, for example, four of their Bf 110s were shot down. But the *Geschwader*'s blackest day was to occur ten days later when the Eighth AF struck at Augsburg. American escort fighters claimed the destruction of 77 Luftwaffe aircraft, with many of them being the hapless Bf 110s of ZG 76. For of the *Geschwader*'s 43 *Zerstörer* aloft on that 16 March, 26 were shot down and another ten crash-landed with varying degrees of damage!

This massacre finally marked the end of the Bf 110's long and less than illustrious career as a daylight *Zerstörer*. In May 1944 I. and II./ZG 76 re-equipped with the Me 410, but this change of equipment made very little difference. Commanded now by Oberstleutnant Robert Kowalewski (a renowned bomber pilot), the *Geschwader*'s casualty lists continued to grow. In July I./ZG 76 converted on to Bf 109s and was redesignated to become I./JG 76.

A reminder of things that were. Confirmation by the OKL of the destruction of a 'Fortress II' at 1235 hrs during the Berlin raid of 6 March 1944. Oberleutnant Schob of 1./ZG 76 is credited with the initial *Herausschuss*. And although the straggling Fortress was subsequently dispatched by Unteroffizier Kurt Anlauf (of the Luftwaffe's Ferry Group 1!), the kill was officially recorded as the 12th victory for 1./ZG 76 (which had been formed in November 1943). Three minutes later, at 1238 hrs, Herbert Schob downed another B-17 on his own to bring the *Staffel*'s collective score to 13. Some seven minutes later still Schob's Bf 110G would be hit by P-51s, resulting in both crew members bailing out wounded

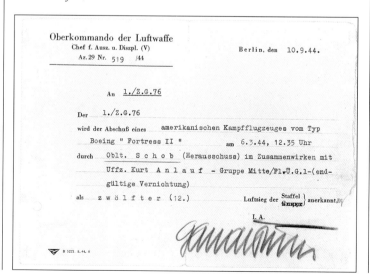

II. *Gruppe*, led by the 'Last of the Prussians', Major Herbert Kaminski (veteran of the Battle of Britain and Crete, Knight's Cross holder and seven-victory *Experte*), stuck it out a few weeks longer as one of the Luftwaffe's last two surviving *Zerstörergruppen*. In August they transferred to Czechoslovakia, and thence up into East Prussia. Based at Seerappen, II./ZG 76 appears to have doubled as a repository for the Luftwaffe's unwanted Me 410s, for on 15 October 1944 they had no fewer than 62 of the twin-engined fighters on strength!

But the end could be postponed no longer. In November II./ZG 76 relinquished their Me 410s and began conversion onto the Fw 190. The intention was for them to form the new II./JG 76. Like so many plans drawn up by the Luftwaffe in the final six months of the war, however, this one failed to materialise. After retraining on the single-seaters, the pilots of II./ZG 76 were dispersed among existing *Jagdgruppen*.

And so, with the single exception of the isolated IV./ZG 26, whose Me 410s would continue to patrol Norwegian coastal waters until February 1945, the *Zerstörerwaffe* was no more. No other arm of the wartime Luftwaffe had had such a chequered, complex and tortuous history as that undergone by Reichsmarschall Göring's once-cherished 'Ironsides'.

Thousands served with the *Zerstörer*. Many were killed. Few are remembered today. But one man epitomises that force and those times. Unteroffizier Herbert Schob's first victory – an I-16 Rata – was scored in Spain on 24 September 1938. He added five more kills during his service with the *Condor Legion*. In World War 2 he flew with I.(Z)/LG 1 in Poland, I./ZG 76 over Norway and in the West, I./ZG 26 in the Balkans and on the Eastern Front, and with I. and II./ZG 76 in Defence of the Reich. On 9 June 1944 Oberleutnant Herbert Schob was awarded the Knight's Cross. He survived the war with a final total of 28 enemy aircraft destroyed, including the six in Spain, one on the Eastern Front and ten four-engined 'heavies'.

Throughout it all, every one of his aircraft from the light grey Bf 109D of his *Legion* days to the heavily-armed *Pulk-Zerstörer* of mid-1944 had carried his personal symbol. A cryptic set of four initials – NNWW, *'Nur Nicht Weich Werden'*... 'Don't Give In'.

Despite being fitted with rockets or 50 mm BK 5 cannon (as on this machine here, which is seen breaking away after a firing pass at a 388th BG Fortress), the Me 410 could not survive in the hostile environment above its own Homeland. The days of the Luftwaffe's twin-engined fighter force had come to an end

Oberleutnant Herbert Schob, seen here in all his finery, enjoyed a wartime career that spanned the history of the *Zerstörerwaffe* from first day until last

APPENDICES

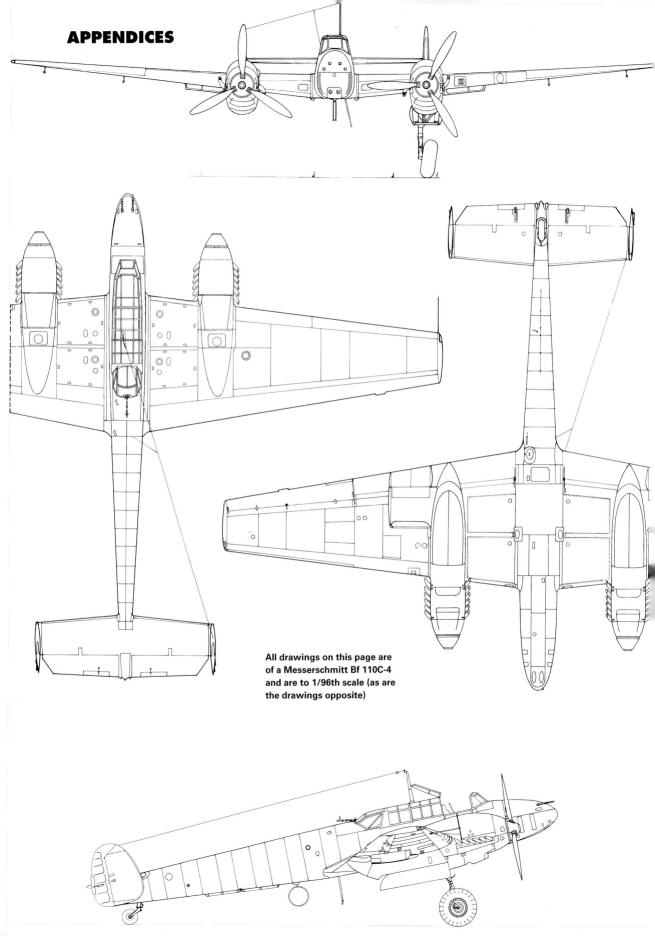

All drawings on this page are
of a Messerschmitt Bf 110C-4
and are to 1/96th scale (as are
the drawings opposite)

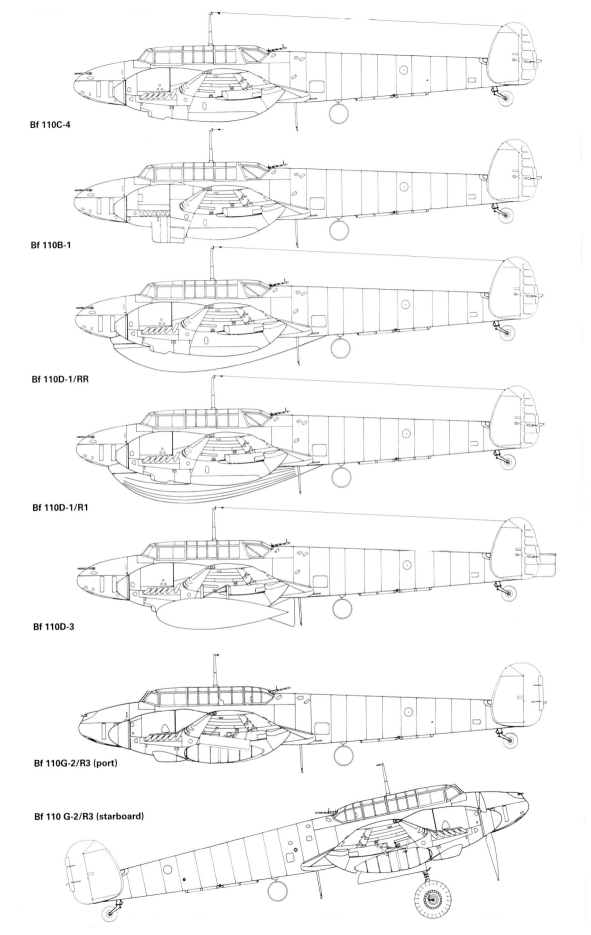

Bf 110C-4

Bf 110B-1

Bf 110D-1/RR

Bf 110D-1/R1

Bf 110D-3

Bf 110G-2/R3 (port)

Bf 110 G-2/R3 (starboard)

COLOUR PLATES

1
Bf 110C 'L1+IH' of Feldwebel Herbert Schob, 1.(Z)/LG 1, Jesau, East Prussia, September 1939

Wearing standard early war camouflage (schwarzgrün 70/dunkelgrün 71 upper surfaces and hellblau 65 undersides) and a textbook set of national insignia of the period, *'Ida-Heinrich'* was the mount of Herbert Schob at the start of the Polish campaign. He downed one of two P.7 fighters which fell to his *Gruppe* on the first morning of hostilities (although he erroneously entered it in his logbook as a P.24). The success was marked with a victory bar below the windshield.

2
Bf 110C 'L1+LK' of Oberleutnant Werner Methfessel, *Staffelkapitän* 14.(Z)/LG 1, Mannheim-Sandhofen, May 1940

Although no *Zerstörer* ace emerged from the Polish campaign, 2. *Staffel's* Werner Methfessel came close with four. He was to claim his fifth during the 'Phoney War', and scored more during the opening phase of the *Blitzkrieg* in the West. By this time the parent *Gruppe* had been redesignated V.(Z)/LG 1, but the three component *Staffeln* (now 13., 14. and 15.) continued to use their original H, K, L identification letters. Note, however, the introduction of 1940-style pattern and position of the national insignia on *'Ludwig-Kurfürst'*.

3
Bf 110C 'L1+IL' of Leutnant Rudolf Altendorf, 15.(Z)/LG 1, Caen-Rocquancourt, July 1940

Altendorf's *'Ida-Ludwig'* is still wearing the early-war camouflage scheme at the start of the Battle of Britain. Note, however, the combination of narrow-bordered fuselage cross and repositioned tail swastika. Another point of interest is the small white, cartoon-style, locomotive and tender carried below the windshield. This is believed to refer back to the then 3. *Staffel's* train-busting activities in Poland. Note that this machine, and the two above, all display spinner tips in their respective *Staffel* colours.

4
Bf 110C '2N+GB' of Hauptmann Wolfgang Falck, Gruppenkommandeur I./ZG 1, Aalborg-West, April 1940

The use of his 'lucky' individual letter 'G' from his earlier days with ZG 26 (see profile 18) may have prompted Falck to add the fighter-style *Kommandeur's* chevrons depicted here just to prove that this really *was* the CO's machine! By current regulations the correct code should have read '2N+AB'. Note the eight victory bars on the fin, the first three being Polish and the last one Danish. Postwar records suggest, however, that Falck scored only seven kills, one of the four intervening RAF claims being unconfirmed.

5
Bf 110C '2N+BB' of Oberleutnant Siegfried Wandam, Gruppenadjutant I./ZG 1, Vendeville, May 1940

In keeping with Falck's double-chevron above, Wandam's aircraft sported the requisite adjutant's symbol ahead of the fuselage code. Note the early-style fuselage cross, and the fact that both machines also had their individual letters – in dark green, outlined in white – repeated on the front of the nose. Wandam achieved no kills as a *Zerstörer* pilot, but went on to score ten in nightfighters. He served first with NJG 1, but was killed in action over Belgium in the early hours of 4 July 1943 as a Hauptmann flying with the Stab of I./NJG 5.

6
Bf 110G 'S9+IC' of Hauptmann Günther Tonne, *Gruppenkommandeur* II./ZG 1, Byelgorod-II, Ukraine, June 1942

This second-generation II./ZG 1 (ex-II./SKG 210) aircraft displays the elaborate 'Wasp' nose which, in fact, dates back to an even earlier period in the unit's existence when it was operating as III./ZG 76 in Norway. Originally designed as a *Gruppe* badge by Richard Marchfelder, and featuring three small wasps over a stylised cloud, it was developed into the striking motif shown here presumably to compete with II./ZG 76's distinctive 'Sharksmouth'. Note the yellow Eastern Front theatre band encircling the fuselage aft of the wing root, and Tonne's tally on the fin –17 victory bars, the last eight bearing Soviet Stars. Appointed *Kommodore* of SKG 10 in December 1942, Major Tonne was killed in Italy on 15 July 1943 when the engine of his Fw 190 failed during take-off from Reggio. His final tally is believed to have numbered at least 20.

7
Bf 110C '3M+AA' of Oberstleutnant Friedrich Vollbracht, *Geschwaderkommodore* ZG 2, Toussus-le-Noble, August 1940

Still bearing early-style fuselage crosses at the height of the Battle of Britain, Vollbracht's *'Anton-Anton'* was 'borrowed' by *Geschwaderadjutant* Oberleutnant Wilhelm Schäfer on 4 September 1940 for a sortie over southern England. Unfortunately – or should that be predictably? – Schäfer fell foul of RAF fighters and was forced to crash-land on Shoreham Downs. Unlike his trusty mount, Oberst Vollbracht survived the war, which he saw out in a succession of training and staff positions. Although not strictly an ace, Vollbracht was one of the few German pilots to score victories in both World Wars, claiming two kills in each conflict.

8
Bf 110C '3U+AA' of Oberstleutnant Johann Schalk, *Geschwaderkommodore* ZG 26, Memmingen, January 1941

Another *Kommodore's* machine, but very different from the previous aircraft. Schalk's Bf 110 wears the mottle finish introduced in 1940. Utilising the brief spell of rest and re-equipment in the Homeland following the Battle of Britain, Schalk has allowed himself a full set of pre-war *Jagdwaffe*-style *Kommodore* markings in *Geschwaderstab* blue (note also the blue and white spinners). He subsequently led ZG 26 during the opening weeks of *Barbarossa*, before assuming command of NJG 3 in August 1941. Schalk's total number of kills is believed to be 21 –11 of them scored in the East.

9
Bf 110E '3U+AB' of Hauptmann Wilhelm Spies, *Gruppenkommandeur* I./ZG 26, Eastern Front, Summer 1941

Similarly finished to *'Anton-Anton'* above, Spies' *'Anton-Berta'* now also sports the yellow markings of the Eastern Front. Having just been awarded the Knight's Cross (on 14 June 1941) for ten victories in the west, Spies has already claimed four Soviet kills, as witness the scoreboard on his tailfin.

10

Bf 110C 'U8+BB' of Hauptmann Günther Specht, *Gruppenadjutant* **I./ZG 26, France, May 1940**

Prominently displaying the *Gruppenstab*'s *Ringelpitz* (Ring o'roses) emblem of two aircraft (a red German 'pike' chasing a black British 'fish') on the nose, this Adjutant's machine also carries below the cockpit a chevron superimposed on a pencil – making quite clear the pilot's feeling about the administrative side of his duties ('*Papierkrieg*', or 'bumph', is the same in every man's air force!). Specht was very much a man of action, and despite losing an eye in an attack on a RAF Wellington over the German Bight in December 1939, he had returned to combat flying, and would be shot down another six times during the course of the war. Transferring to single-seaters and rising to command JG 11, Major Günther Specht was finally posted missing during Operation *Bodenplatte*, the *Jagdwaffe*'s New Year's Day attack on Allied airfields on 1 January 1945. With a final score of 34, he too would receive a posthumous Knight's Cross and promotion to Oberstleutnant.

11

Bf 110E '3U+BC' of Hauptmann Ralph von Rettberg, *Gruppenkommandeur* **II./ZG 26, Suwalki, June 1941**

Yet another machine in mottle finish, this one also bears unit markings. The *Geschwader* emblem on the nose is a stylised 'HW' (the initials of Horst Wessel, the Nazi 'martyr' after whom ZG 26 was officially named – and, unofficially, largely ignored!) on a red-and-black quartered shield. The white clog on the port engine cowling is the badge of II. *Gruppe*. Carrying *Geschwaderadjutant* codes, this was not von Rettberg's own aircraft, but one he is recorded as having often flown. He survived the war with a score of eight enemy aircraft shot down and 12 destroyed on the ground.

12

Bf 110E '3U+AC' of Hauptmann Werner Thierfelder, *Gruppenkommandeur* **II./ZG 26, Smolensk, January 1942**

This aircraft of von Rettberg's successor reflects the *Gruppe*'s increasing involvement in ground-support operations. No sign of unit badges here. In their place, an overall white scribble camouflage to break up the silhouette of the low-flying Bf 110s. Thierfelder later briefly commanded III. *Gruppe* in Defence of the Reich, and then oversaw its transition into a jet trials unit. He was killed while flying an Me 262 west of Munich on 18 July 1944. His final score was 27, the majority of which had been claimed on the Eastern Front, as were the 41 additional aircraft destroyed on the ground.

13

Bf 110C '3U+AN' of Oberleutnant Theodor Rossiwall, *Staffelkapitän* **5./ZG 26, St Trond, May 1940**

Back to the Battle of France with this standard dark green/black green machine, the mount of the new *Staffelkapitän* of 5./ZG 26, already proudly displaying five victory bars on the tailfin. Note that the 'Ace of Spades' was not the sole property of the famous JG 53 – it was also used by this *Zerstörerstaffel* as a unit marking. After a spell on nightfighters (with both NGJs 1 and 4), Rossiwall returned to the *Zerstörer* as *Kommodore* of the 'new' ZG 76 in 1943. He survived the war with a final total of 17 kills, including two by night and three 'heavies' downed in Defence of the Reich.

14

Bf 110D '3U+AD' of Hauptmann Georg Christl, *Gruppenkommandeur* **III./ZG 26, North Africa, January 1942**

'*Anton-Dora*', flown by Christl at the start of his long tenure of command of III./ZG 26 in the Mediterranean and North Africa, sports a typical brown-green dapple camouflage finish and a standard set of white theatre markings. Awarded the Knight's Cross for leadership of the *Gruppe* in the desert (his personal score then stood at just three kills), Major Christl was later posted to Parchim for the last ten months of the war to head *Jagdgruppe* 10, an experimental unit testing specialised anti-bomber weapons. His own final tally stood at seven.

15

Bf 110E '3U+AR' of Oberleutnant Georg Christl, *Staffelkapitän* **of 7./ZG 26, Taranto, Italy, April 1941**

Prior to assuming command of III./ZG 26, Georg Christl had served as the *Kapitän* of 7. *Staffel*. Having arrived in Sicily by the beginning of 1941, the *Gruppe*'s aircraft were already wearing Mediterranean theatre markings when they were called upon to participate in the invasion of Yugoslavia the following spring. Hence the combination illustrated here of white fuselage band together with the yellow cowlings and rudders worn by units taking part in the Balkans campaign.

16

Bf 110E '3U+FR' of Oberleutnant Alfred Wehmeyer, *Staffelkapitän* **of 7./ZG 26, Derna, May 1942**

Joining II. *Gruppe* at the height of the Battle of Britain, Wehmeyer was appointed *Staffelkapitän* of 7./JG 26 in June 1942. By this time the exigencies of the war in the desert meant that crews were flying whichever aircraft was available and/or serviceable. One often used by Wehmeyer was '*Friedrich-Richard*', but he was killed in '3U+HR'.

17

Bf 110C 'M8+DH' of Leutnant Helmut Lent, 1./ZG 76, Jever, December 1939

Lent's '*Dora-Heinrich*' is in textbook 1939 finish and markings, including narrow-proportioned fuselage cross and tail swastika positioned across both fin and rudder. The four victory bars include the three Wellingtons claimed on 18 December in the 'Battle of the German Bight', one of which was subsequently disallowed. After scoring eight confirmed kills by day, Lent transferred to the nightfighter arm.

18

Bf 110C 'M8-GK' of Hauptmann Wolfgang Falck, *Staffelkapitän* **2./ZG 76, Jever, December 1939**

Almost identical to Lent's machine, Falck's differs only in detail – red 2, *Staffel* trim, six victory bars (three Polish, three British) and a *Staffel* badge below the cockpit, the latter depicting a red ladybird on a white shield. Note, however, that Falck has already adopted his 'lucky' letter 'G', although regulations (then still strictly enforced) laid down that a *Staffelkapitän* should fly aircraft 'A'. Undeterred, Falck took 'G' with him to ZG 1 and thence into the *Nachtjagdwaffe*.

19

Bf 110C 'M8+HK' of Oberfeldwebel Leo Schuhmacher, 2./ZG 76, Stavanger, August 1940

By the time 2./ZG 76 were stationed in Norway, most of their aircraft, including Wk-Nr 3170 seen here, were carrying new style national insignia (wider fuselage crosses, repositioned tail swastikas). Individual details include the *Staffel*'s ladybird badge, four victory bars and the unusual presentation of the aircraft's individual letter 'H'. Note, too, the early type of jettisonable fuel tank under the fuselage. Leo Schuhmacher subsequently transferred to single-seaters, serving with JGs 1 and 11 in Defence of the Reich, and finally with the Me 262-equipped JV 44. He claimed his 23rd, and last, kill in March 1945, shortly after being awarded the Knight's Cross.

20

Bf 110D 'M8+AL' of Oberleutnant Gordon Mc Gollob, *Staffelkapitän* 3./ZG 76, Stavanger, August 1940.

One of the unloved *'Dackelbäuche'* ('Dachshund-bellies') which took part in the raid across the North Sea on 15 August 1940. Of 21 Bf 110Ds despatched, seven were lost and two returned to base damaged. Gollob's *'Anton-Ludwig'* was one of the latter. The *'Dackelbauch'* was a failure, being almost immediately replaced by the jettisonable-type tank shown above, which was cleared for use by later mark Bf 110s.

21

Bf 110C 'M8+AC' of Major Erich Groth, *Gruppenkommandeur* II./ZG 76, Abbeville-Yvrench, September 1940

Arguably the most famous, and certainly the best known, Bf 110 unit marking of all was II./ZG 76's distinctive 'Sharksmouth'. Here, it brightens up an otherwise textbook drab machine of the Battle of Britain period. Although assigned to, and normally flown by, the *Gruppenkommandeur* (the five kill bars on the tailfin are believed to be his), *'Anton-Cäsar'* was being piloted by *Gruppenadjutant* Oberleutnant Hermann Weeber when it made an unscheduled belly-landing in a farm garden south of Tunbridge Wells on 4 September

22

Bf 110D 'M8+AC' of Major Erich Groth, *Gruppenkommandeur* II./ZG 76, Stavanger, August 1941

Another 'Sharksmouth' bearing Major Groth's markings was this densely-mottled machine fitted with 300 litre underwing tanks. Note also the yellow wingtips and rudders, the latter possibly serving to identify aircraft of the *Gruppenstab*. Awarded the Knight's Cross on 1 October 1940 with his score on 12, 'Grotze' Groth was to have been appointed Walter Grabmann's successor as *Geschwader-kommodore* of ZG 76, but he was killed in a crash near Stavanger on 11 August 1941 when flying on instruments in bad weather.

23

Bf 110D of *Sonderkommando* Junck (4./ZG 76), Mosul, Iraq, May 1941

As none of the dozen Bf 110s of 4./ZG 76 sent to Iraq carried any individual markings, it is not possible to match a particular aircraft to any one pilot – presumably the serviceability and/or availability of both items was the guiding factor! One pilot known to have claimed a kill in Iraq was future nightfighter *Experte*, and Oak Leaves recipient, Major Martin Drewes. This profile illustrates the salient points of the *Staffel*'s Bf 110s during their short-lived sojourn in the Middle East – the retention of the 'Sharksmouth', the crude overpainting of

the fuselage codes and Luftwaffe markings, the application of Iraqi insignia and the use of 900-litre underwing tanks necessitated by the long distances involved in the operation.

24

Bf 110G '2N+AM' of Oberleutnant Helmut Haugk, *Staffelkapitän* 4./ZG 76, Ansbach, March 1944

A typical 'second generation' Bf 110 in its ultimate guise as a fully-loaded *'Pulk-Zerstörer'*, Haugk's *'Anton-Martha'* displays 1944-style finish and markings, and is encumbered with ventral cannon pack, jettisonable fuel tanks and four underwing rocket launchers. Note also the armoured windshield. 4./ZG 76 was one of the *Staffeln* most heavily hit in the catastrophic air battle of 16 March 1944 (the 'swan song of the Bf 110 *Zerstörer*'), with ten out of Haugk's twelve aircraft being shot down! The *Staffelkapitän* and his *Bordfunker* parachuted to safety, the former going on to command training units for the last year of the war. His final tally of 18 victories included six heavy bombers.

25

Bf 110C 'M8+AP' of Hauptmann Heinz Nacke, *Staffelkapitän* 6./ZG 76, Argos, May 1941

Having spent the winter of 1940/41 patrolling the North Sea, II./ZG 76 were hurriedly transferred south in the spring to take part in the invasion of Crete. Heinz Nacke's *'Anton-Paula'* reflects the move to sunnier climes – standard post-Battle of Britain camouflage finish combined with yellow Balkan campaign markings. Nacke survived the war after commanding a succession of units (operational, experimental and training), but by its end had added no further kills to the 12 which had won him the Knight's Cross on 2 November 1940.

26

Bf 110C 'M8+NP' of Oberleutnant Hans-Joachim Jabs, 6./ZG 76, France, May 1940

Representative of the 'Sharksmouths' at the height of their power, Jab's machine, in textbook finish and markings, is depicted during the *Gruppe*'s headlong advance across France in the late spring/early summer of 1940. The first six kills are already displayed on the tailfin.

27

Bf 110C 'M8+IP' of Oberleutnant Hans-Joachim Jabs, 6./ZG 76, German Bight, Winter 1940-41

By the close of the Battle of Britain Jab's score had risen to 19 (for which he was awarded the Knight's Cross on 1 October 1940). These are seen faithfully recorded on the fin of *'Ida-Paula'* (Wk-Nr 3866) the following winter. Jabs retrained on nightfighters in September 1941. He spent the remainder of the war with NJG 1, rising to become *Geschwaderkommodore*, winning the Oak Leaves and adding another 31 kills in the process (two of the latter, incidentally, were claimed by day – a brace of Spitfires on 29 April 1944).

28

Bf 110D '2N+DP' of Feldwebel Hans Peterburs, 6./ZG 76, Stavanger, Winter 1940-41

Also sent to patrol the North Sea after the Battle of Britain, III./ZG 76 operated over Norwegian coastal waters. Two points of interest here. Despite its redesignation six months earlier, the *Gruppe* was still using fuselage codes introduced during its previous service as II./ZG 1 (a practice which, it is believed, was continued up until the unit's further redesignation as II./SKG 210 in May 1941). Note also the original form of the *Gruppe* badge. Hans Peterburs served with the *Gruppe* throughout its identity changes between 1939-43. Transferring to the ground-attack arm and II./SG 4, he was killed in action against RAF fighters over Salerno, Italy, on 11 January 1944. His aerial tally totalled at least 20, with another 30+ destroyed on the ground in Russia.

29

Bf 110E 'LN+FR' of Oberleutnant Felix Maria Brandis, *Staffelkapitän* 1.(Z)/JG 77, Rovaniemi, Finland, September 1941

As a semi-autonomous *Zerstörerstaffel* attached to a *Jagdgeschwader*, 1.(Z)/JG 77 devised its own four-letter unit code: 'LN' to the right of the fuselage cross, with the individual aircraft letter immediately to its left, followed by 'R'. The *Staffelkapitän*'s aircraft illustrates this clearly, together with the unit badge, a typical grey finish and the pilot's victory tally – currently standing at eight – on the tailfin (note that the line of kill bars are parallel to the ground when the aircraft is at rest, not aligned to the machine's horizontal axis).

30

Bf 110C 'LN+IR' of Feldwebel Theodor Weissenberger, 1.(Z)/JG 77, Kirkenes, Norway, September 1941

Similar to the machine above, but minus the victory bars (Weissenberger had yet to make his mark!), *'Ida-Richard'* also wears the *Staffel* badge – a Dachshund with an I-16 *Rata* in its jaws. Throughout its various changes of designation, the unit was known to all and sundry simply as the *'Dackel' Staffel* (it was Brandis' pet, whom he named 'Lockheed' after his first victory – a Hudson off Norway – who modelled for the badge). Having scored 23 *Zerstörer* kills, Weissenberger transferred to the *Staffel*'s then parent *Geschwader* (JG 5) in September 1942, and flew single-seaters for the rest of the war. He ended it on the Me 262 as *Kommodore* of JG 7, with the Oak Leaves and a final total of 208 victories. Theodor Weissenberger lost his life in an accident while racing at the Nürburgring on 10 June 1950.

31

Bf 110E 'S9+AH' of Oberleutnant Wolfgang Schenk, *Staffelkapitän* 1./SKG 210, Sechinskaya, September 1941

Illustrating the pitfalls of accurate unit identification, this aircraft displays almost identical markings to the machine of II./ZG 1 depicted in profile 6. Only the pilot's personal scoreboard on the fin and rudder (15 kills plus 5 tanks) offers a clue as to the date – September 1941 – thus placing it firmly in the middle of the *Gruppe*'s eight months existence as II./SKG 210 (May 1941-January 1942). Wolfgang Schenk was another who later flew Me 262s, in his case as a fighter-bomber pilot and the *Führer* of the *Einsatzkommando* Schenk.

FIGURE PLATES

1

Oberleutnant Werner Methfessel of 14.(Z)./LG 1 at Würzburg in the winter of 1939-40. Having claimed four kills in Poland, 'ace-in-waiting' Methfessel spent the ensuing winter of the 'Phoney War' with his *Staffel* at Würzburg. He is seen here wrapped up against the cold, hands deep in the side pockets of his one-piece, zippered, fur-collared flying suit. Flying boots, officer's pattern belt and side-cap complete the ensemble.

2

Hauptmann Heinz Nacke, *Staffelkapitän* of 6./ZG 76, at Jever, Winter 1940-41. Looking altogether nattier the following winter, Nacke is shown wearing his 'trademark' sheepskin jacket (with Hauptmann sleeve patches), together with breeches and boots. Note the white scarf and the Knight's Cross, the latter awarded at the close of the Battle of Britain for 12 kills.

3

Oberfeldwebel Richard Heller of III./ZG 26, Mediterranean theatre, September 1941. Also sporting a recently received Knight's Cross (awarded on 21 August 1941), Heller's outfit reflects his *Gruppe*'s transfer to the Mediterranean and North Africa – one-piece lightweight zippered flying overalls (again with rank patches on the sleeves), inflatable life-jacket and high-visibility yellow helmet cover, the last two items being essential accoutrements for long overwater patrols.

4

Hauptmann Theodor Rossiwall, *Staffelkapitän* of 5./ZG 26 on the Eastern Front, Autumn 1941. A third recent Knight's Cross recipient, Rossiwall is depicted wearing standard officer's service dress of tunic and breeches, together with the Schirmmütze (officer's peaked cap). His decorations in this period include an operational flight clasp and medal ribbons above the left breast pocket, Iron Cross with wound badge and pilot's 'wings' below, and the War Service Cross on the right pocket.

5

Oberleutnant Felix Maria Brandis, *Staffelkapitän* of 1.(Z)./JG 77 at Rovaniemi, Winter 1941-42. More suitably attired for Eastern Front service, particularly above the Arctic Circle, Brandis' all-white winter garb comprises a fur-collared, lined and padded jacket and zippered trousers, plus standard issue fur cap, shown here with the earflaps down. Note the black rank patches (two 'moustaches' and bar of an Oberleutnant) conspicuous against the white of Brandis' buttoned sleeve.

6

Major Eduard Tratt, *Gruppenkommandeur* of II./ZG 26 at Hildesheim, Autumn 1943. Although not known whether he actually wore it in combat himself, Tratt is depicted here in the SF 30 steel helmet issued to the crews of his *Zerstörergruppe*. Intended to protect the wearer against fire from US bombers, the SF 30 had no fastenings of its own, but was reportedly simply jammed down hard on the standard flying helmet beneath it! Unsurprisingly, perhaps, it did not see widespread service.

BIBLIOGRAPHY

DIERICH, WOLFGANG, *Die Verbände der Luftwaffe*. Motorbuch Verlag, Stuttgart, 1976

EIMANNSBERGER, LUDWIG v., *Zerstörergruppe: A History of V.(Z)/LG 1 – I./NJG 3, 1939-41*. Schiffer Military History, Atglen, 1998

GIRBIG, WERNER, *Jagdgeschwader 5 "Eismeerjäger"*. Motorbuch Verlag, Stuttgart, 1976

GOSS, CHRIS, *Bloody Biscay: The History of V./KG 40*. Crécy, 1997

GRABLER, JOSEF, *Mit Bomben und MGs über Polen*. Verlag Bertelsmann, Gütersloh, 1942

GROEHLER, OLAF, *Kampf um die Luftherrschaft*. Militärverlag der DDR, Berlin, 1988

HELD, WERNER, *Die deutsche Tagjagd*. Motorbuch Verlag, Stuttgart, 1977

HELD, WERNER, *Reichsverteidigung: Die deutsche Tagjagd 1943-1945*. Podzun-Pallas, Friedberg, 1988

HELD, WERNER/OBERMEIER, ERNST, *Die deutsche Luftwaffe im Afrika-Feldzug 1941-1943*. Motorbuch Verlag, Stuttgart

ISHOVEN, ARMAND VAN, *Messerschmitt Bf 110 at War*. Ian Allan, London, 1985

KAUFMANN, JOHANNES, *Meine Flugberichte 1935-1945*. Journal Verlag Schwend, Schwäbisch Hall, 1989

LOEWENSTERN, ERICH v., *Luftwaffe über dem Feind*. Wilhem Limpert-Verlag, Berlin, 1941

MATTHIAS, JOACHIM, *Alarm! Deutsche Flieger über England*. Steiniger-Verlage, Berlin, 1940

MEHNERT, KURT und TEUBER, REINHARD, *Die Deutsche Luftwaffe 1939-1945*. Militär-Verlag Patzwall, Norderstedt, 1996

NAUROTH, HOLGER, *Die deutsche Luftwaffe vom Nordkap bis Tobruk 1939-1945*. Podzun-Pallas Verlag, Friedberg

NAUROTH, HOLGER/HELD, WERNER, *Messerschmitt Bf 110 Zerstörer an allen Fronten 1939-1945*. Motorbuch Verlag, Stuttgart, 1978

NEITZEL, SÖNKE, *Der Einsatz der deutschen Luftwaffe über dem Atlantik und der Nordsee, 1939-1945*. Bernard & Graefe Verlag, Bonn, 1995

NOWARRA, HEINZ J., *Luftwaffen- Einsatz "Barbarossa" 1941*. Podzun-Pallas Verlag, Friedberg

OBERMAIER, ERNST, *Die Ritterkreuzträger der Luftwaffe 1939-1945, Band I Jagdflieger*. Verlag Dieter Hoffmann, Mainz, 1966

OFFICIAL, *The Rise and Fall of the German Air Force (1933 to 1945)*. Air Ministry, London, 1948

OKW, *Der Sieg in Polen*, Zeitgeschichte-Verlag. Berlin, 1939

OKW, *Sieg über Frankreich*, Zeitgeschichte-Verlag. Berlin, 1940

OKW, *Kampf um Norwegen*, Zeitgeschichte-Verlag. Berlin, 1940

OKW, *Fahrten und Flüge gegen England*. Zeitgeschichte-Verlag, Berlin, 1941

OKW, *Die Wehrmacht - Das Buch des Krieges 1939-1940*

OKW, *Die Wehrmacht - Das Buch des Krieges 1940-1941*

OKW, *Die Wehrmacht - Das Buch des Krieges 1942*

OKW, *Wehrmachtberichte Weltgeschichte*. Verlag "Die Wehrmacht", Berlin, 1941

PLOCHER, Genltn. HERMANN, *The German Air Force versus Russia, 1942*. Arno Press, New York, 1966

PRICE, ALFRED, *Battle of the Britain: The Hardest Day, 18 August 1940*. Macdonald and Jane's, London, 1979

PRICE, ALFRED, *Battle of Britain Day, 15 September 1940*. Sidgwick & Jackson, London, 1990

RAMSEY, WINSTON G. (ed.), *The Battle of Britain Then and Now*. After the Battle, London, 1985 (3rd edition)

RAMSEY, WINSTON G. (ed.), *The Blitz Then and Now (Vols. 1 & 2)*. After the Battle, London, 1987 and 1988

RIES jr., KARL, *Dora Kurfürst und rote 13, Vols. I-IV*. Verlag Dieter Hoffman, Finthen/Mainz, 1964-69

RIES jr., KARL, *Markings and Camouflage Systems of Luftwaffe Aircraft in World War II, Vols. I-IV*. Verlag Dieter Hoffman, Finthen/Mainz, 1963-72

RIES jr., KARL, *Photo Collection/Luftwaffe Embleme 1939-1945*. Verlag Dieter Hoffman, Finthen/Mainz, 1976

RIES jr., KARL/OBERMEIER, ERNST. Bilanz am Seitenleitwerk, Verlag Dieter Hoffman, 1970

RLM, *Jahrbuch der deutschen Luftwaffe 1940*. Verlag von Breitkopf & Härtel, Leipzig, 1940

ROSSIWALL, THEODOR, *Fliegerlegende*. Kurt Vowinckel Verlag, Neckargemünd, 1964

SCHRAMM, PERCY E. (ed.), *Kriegstagebuch des OKW (8 Vols.)*. Manfred Pawlak, Herrsching, 1982

SHORES, CHRISTOPHER, *Air Aces*. Bison Books, Greenwich, 1983

SHORES, CHRISTOPHER, *Duel for the Sky*. Grub Street, London, 1985

SHORES, CHRISTOPHER/RING, HANS, *Fighters over the Desert*. Neville Spearman, London, 1969

SHORES, CHRISTOPHER, et al., *Fighters over Tunisia*. Neville Spearman, London, 1975

SHORES, CHRISTOPHER, et al., *Air War for Yugoslavia, Greece and Crete 1940-1941*. Grub Street, London, 1987

SHORES, CHRISTOPHER, et al., *Fledgling Eagles*. Grub Street, London, 1991

SMITH, J. R. & GALLASPY, J. D., *Luftwaffe Camouflage and Markings 1935-1945, Vol. 2*. Kookaburra Technical Publications, Melbourne, 1976

SMITH, PETER & WALKER, EDWIN, *War in the Aegean*. William Kimber, London, 1974

SUPF, PETER, *Luftwaffe schlägt zu!* Im Deutschen Verlag, Berlin, 1939

SUPF, PETER, *Luftwaffe von Sieg zu Sieg: Von Norwegen bis Kreta*. Im Deutschen Verlag, Berlin, 1941

VARIOUS, *Unsere Flieger über Polen*. Im Deutschen Verlag, Berlin, 1941

VASCO, JOHN, J. and CORNWALL, PETER D., *Zerstörer, The Messerschmitt 110 and its Units in 1940*. JAC Publications, Norwich, 1995

VÖLKER, KARL-HEINZ, *Die deutsche Luftwaffe 1933-1939*. Deutsche Verlags-Anstalt, Stuttgart, 1967

WAKEFIELD, KENNETH, *Luftwaffe Encore: A Study of Two Attacks in September 1940*. William Kimber, London, 1979

WIDFELDT, BO, *The Luftwaffe in Sweden 1939-1945*. Monogram, Boylston, 1983

WUNDSHAMMER, BENNO, *Flieger – Ritter – Helden: Mit dem Haifischgeschwader in Frankreich*. Verlag Bertelsmann, Gütersloh, 1942

MAGAZINES AND PERIODICALS (VARIOUS ISSUES)

Adler, Der
Aeroplane, The
Berliner Illustrierte Zeitung
Flight
Flug-Revue International
Flugzeug
Flugzeug Archiv
Jägerblatt

Jet & Prop
Jet & Prop Archiv
Signal